Hitoshi Nomura

1970. 3.29. 16:01
Iodine
1970. 3.29. 15:36
Iodine
1970. 3.29. 15:03
Iodine
1970. 3. 29. 14:21
Iodine
1970. 3. 29. 13:45
Iodine
1970. 3. 29. 13:18
Iodine
1970. 3. 29. 12:30
Iodine

Hitoshi Nomura

Early Works
Sculpture, Photography, Film, Sound

Martha Buskirk

Reiko Tomii

McCAFFREY FINE ART

Note to the Reader

Japanese and other East Asian names are
given in the traditional order, surname first.
Exceptions are made in the case of individuals
who primarily reside outside their native
countries *and* adopt the Western system.

Contents

Figure 1. Creating *Dryice*, 1969

An Interview with Nomura Hitoshi
by Fergus McCaffrey

Kyoto, Japan, April 20, 2010

Fergus McCaffrey: What inspired you to become an artist?

Nomura Hitoshi: Well, the answer depends on what you think an artist is. . . . [laughs] If the question is, "What made me an artist?" then I have to ask you, "What do you think an artist is? At what point does someone become an artist?" I don't think you would call someone an artist just because they made something. . . .

McCaffrey: Well, let me change the question slightly, then. Why did you go to art school instead of, for example, studying science?

Nomura: Well, that's because . . . that's fate, if you will, or I should say I succumbed to temptation. . . . [laughs] Let's see, my home was very Japanese; my family cherished Japanese tradition. Drinking tea meant tea ceremony. My mother played the *koto*. Our *tansu* chests were filled with hanging scrolls [*jiku*] and unmounted fragments of ink drawings. That's the kind of environment I grew up in.

While studying alone late at night, I'd look in those chests and see these rolled-up unmounted drawings. I was probably a high school student, and I started thinking that it would be really interesting if I could draw like that. Until then, I was more or less good at

science. That's why I said that I succumbed to temptation: I really wanted to draw like that. So, in my last year of high school, I studied drawing for the first time, and the drawings I did of plaster busts in class were the first and last academic charcoal drawings I made in my entire career. That's how it started.

McCaffrey: Between 1968 and 1969, you made an eight-meter-tall sculpture out of stacked cardboard boxes, called *Tardiology*. Later in 1969, you worked with dry ice, and then with iodine in 1970. These are very unorthodox substances to make sculpture from. How did you start working with materials like these?

Nomura: Yes, cardboard was the first material I used, and that experience led me to use dry ice and iodine. My use of cardboard derived from eight transparent plastic capsules I had made in 1968 [called *Untitled* and shown at Akiyama Gallery, Tokyo, and the first *Exhibition of Contemporary Plastic Art*, in Kyoto's Okazaki Park]. Each capsule was ninety centimeters in diameter and large enough for a person to get in. I asked a professional plastic fabricator to make these forms for me, but they found it difficult, so I ended up somehow making them myself. Because of the difficulty of making these sculptures, I wanted to preserve them,

although they were large and I had no place to store them. So rather than destroying them, I decided to have eight special cardboard boxes made to protect and store the sculptures. They were too large to store in my room, so I stacked these under the eaves of my apartment building, wrapped in plastic. They were somewhat protected; however, they were exposed to a certain amount of wind, rain, and humidity. Plus the capsules were heavy, with each one weighing about thirty kilograms, and so the stack started to collapse. When I saw them disintegrating, I had a very strong reaction, probably because these cardboard boxes contained something dear to my heart: "Oh my god, they're collapsing! What the hell am I going to do now?" At first I had a negative reaction.

In the sculpture department at Kyoto City University of Arts, we learned how to make beautiful, interesting forms. We were taught that sculptors were supposed to make these forms. But I was looking at this collapsing structure that troubled me a lot. It was the first time to see such a form with my own eye, and I had to reckon that it was completely different from what we had learned at school. It was "bad" and caused me a headache, but a form nonetheless. So it got me thinking, "Why can't I, as an artist, accept it as something positive, instead of thinking negatively? Why do we have to deny it?"

These were some of the questions that arose in my mind. It wasn't right away, naturally, as I was more concerned about what I was going to do if the whole thing collapsed. But after a while, after I calmed down, I took a look at it and it was a form. This collapsing stack of storage boxes was a big impetus for me and led me to make *Tardiology*.

McCaffrey: How did your professors react to your use of unusual materials?

Nomura: In the sculpture department, we were given different materials and different projects every six months, so that we'd get experience with each one. For example, we did stone carving—not marble, but granite—for six months, and then for the next six months we did wood carving with big blocks of wood, and so on. That was the curriculum. We never were instructed to make things a certain way. Nobody would say anything. It was that kind of school. They taught us how to make stone chisels, like a blacksmith, and things like that, but other than that we were just supposed to learn by watching what the teachers were doing. If we asked a question, naturally they would answer us, but for the most part the teachers never told us what to do. We watched them working, and just figured it out by watching them. It was the same with our year-end and graduation projects. Especially with graduation works, we could choose whatever material we wanted. So when I chose to use cardboard, none of the teachers at the time were involved in my decision to use that material or what I intended to do with it. Things are different nowadays, however.

McCaffrey: Can you talk about the first presentation of *Tardiology* and the reaction?

Nomura: When I was preparing the large cardboard boxes that made up *Tardiology*, no one was really aware of my sculptural presentation. So only when I started assembling them at Kyoto Municipal Museum of Art, where all of the school's year-end and graduation projects were presented, did the professors come to learn what I was up to. When it was completed, they said, "Whoa, isn't it dangerous?" The teachers reacted strongly when the museum authorities complained—that it was unseemly because cardboard was used to make shipping boxes. They didn't think that it was a suitable material for a work of art . . . though I'm second-guessing what they thought here. Also this tall structure, eight or ten meters, looked rickety, although I used wires to stabilize it. Once it was up, the museum requested me to dismantle it right away. So I told the junior students that the museum wanted to get rid of the sculpture, and that I wasn't going to let that happen, and we placed wires around it. However, Professor Tsuji Shindō, the department head at the university, said that everything would be OK. He was the only one who sided with me, and because of his intervention, it stayed there.

The reaction of people was important, but I didn't go around asking people what they thought. I had already heard one opinion, when I installed it: "Take it down! It's dangerous!" So I had already received the opinion that sculptures are things that are supposed to stand firm. That was the conceptual framework through which people traditionally viewed sculpture. And my purpose in presenting *Tardiology* was to say, "There's another way."

McCaffrey: Was *Tardiology* conceived as a sculpture to be experienced in its physicality, or through photography?

Nomura: Well, I made the piece, and the point was to watch the process. Traditionally, after a work of art is installed, it's completed. Then all you have to do is to look at it. To the viewer, the appearance would remain unchanged from beginning to end. But what I thought at the time was that the moment of installation marked the starting point. Then, because of gravity, the wind, rain, and time, it would gradually fall apart. *Tardiology* wouldn't have been complete if it hadn't fallen apart. It was an artwork designed to change over time, meaning that it would be impossible to view it in the way we conventionally see sculpture—just take a glance at it, and that's enough. Those were all the factors I had in my mind at the time. Taking photographs was important because this work of art was going to collapse and fall apart, and after that happened there would be nothing left.

The sculpture had to stand up at first, and then it had to collapse, but there was no way to rehearse this, as the structure was so big. I wondered, "What would I experience as this was collapsing? Will this actually qualify as a sculpture?" It was something totally new to me, and as far as I was aware, nobody had ever seen anything like it before. I was presenting this as a work of art, and personally I had no doubts that it merited that designation, but I had never seen something like this before, so I couldn't say for sure one way or another. I had no idea how other people who viewed it would react.

In terms of your question about experiencing the work in person or through photography, there were two steps in the evolution of my thinking; I had two experiences. The actual experience of seeing the work collapse in front of me was satisfying. Then, upon developing the pictures of the process of collapse, I received a second level of satisfaction. I really didn't give the act of photographing the process too much thought initially, or whether anybody would think that the photographs were good or not.

What I learned from the photography of *Tardiology* is seen in *Dryice* and *Iodine*.

One of the things I've forgotten to say is that the traditional raison d'être of sculptures was to create monumental commemorative objects—bronze sculptures celebrating victory in war, etc.—which would last longer than a human life. But what I was most interested in when I made my graduation work was this: if a sculpture doesn't have this kind of monumental permanence as its primary goal, is there any reason for it to exist? On the one hand, I had seen the cardboard boxes stored at my apartment collapse; on the other hand, I had this question inside me; and that was probably why I reacted so strongly at that time to the sight of the collapsing boxes. That's why I decided to present as my graduation project something that lacked permanence.

McCaffrey: I've heard many explanations from Western writers that relate the raw materiality and temporality of much of Japanese sculpture in the late 1960s and early 1970s to critical theories such as *wabi-sabi* and the phenomenon of the rebuilding of the Ise Shrine in identical form every twenty years. I think that much of this is outright projection, which has no basis in the day-to-day experience of being an artist in Japan during the period. It strikes me that the prevailing conditions of the Japanese art world were a much more salient influence.

We tend to take the American experience as par for the course, but I was thinking about how very, very unusual it was that during the 1960s and 1970s, there were Leo Castelli and Virginia Dwan making exhibitions and offering stipends to artists who were making largely unsalable work; how collectors like Heiner Friedrich and Philippa de Menil and Giuseppe Panza di Biumo supported such enormously ambitious projects; and how artists reacted to the availability of vast warehouses and tracts of land to make and permanently install their work. It seems to me quite unprecedented and unlike anything that was available to artists in Japan. Here, galleries tended to be rental galleries, the culture was—to quote Reiko Tomii—"to show" as there were no collectors, space was in short supply, and storage was impractically expensive. I was thinking that these factors are surely more significant in the temporality and choice of materials by artists like you than aesthetics and Shinto tradition.

Nomura: I think this comment is important, and I have never heard anyone point out that these types of differences existed in terms of approach, and in terms of the basis for creating works of art. I suppose that's natural, since this is an interview with a Japanese person. I'd never heard that there is anything particular about Japan in this regard. That said, listening to you say these things—and I don't know much about Europe, but hearing about the U.S., I realize that a Japanese artist's attitude might be different when making a work of art. I've never been in contact with the kind of situation that you describe, so I don't exactly know the differences, but I think what you pointed out is extremely important. Art is the kind of thing where, whether you're going to resist or accept the environment that the artist is placed in, the influence of that environment is extremely influential. This is an interesting way of looking at Japanese art from the '60s and early '70s. . . .

McCaffrey: *Tardiology* and *Dryice* document the collapse and evaporation of the high modernist forms of the stack and the cube. You've discussed *Tardiology* in anti-monumental terms. Were these sculptures conceived as challenges to the minimalism of Donald Judd, Tony Smith, or others?

Nomura: The reason I used rectangular forms for *Tardiology* was because of the cubic cardboard boxes that I had seen collapse before.

Another thing I thought at the time was that you could more vividly perceive the deformation if it starts off with straight edges that were clearly visible, with vertical and horizontal lines, that would reveal the slightest changes. If the forms were curved or asymmetrical, it would have looked different. As regards minimalism, I knew about it in 1966 and 1967, when Judd's works were introduced to Japan, but I didn't really have it in mind. More than that, what determined my choice was the fact that I wanted to make the collapse, the gradual deformation, more clearly visible.

McCaffrey: The years 1968–69 were a very politically charged time in Japan, the United States, and in Europe. Contemporaries of yours like Haraguchi Noriyuki adopted a minimalist vocabulary infused with a very political intent. The collapse of structures could be read as having political connotations. Was this the case in your work?

Nomura: Not really. My work from this period doesn't contain anything that was intentionally designed to express something like that. It's not that I'm not interested in those things, but I just didn't include them in my work.

McCaffrey: You consciously chose to take your own photographs of your sculptures, unlike other Japanese sculptors of the period who had professional photographers document their installations. This indicates to me an early acceptance of photography as "art" and the realization of the artistic potential of its practice.

Nomura: In March of 1970, there was the *Kyoto Independent Exhibition* at the Kyoto Municipal Museum of Art, and the critic Nakahara Yūsuke came and critiqued it. I exhibited *Dryice* and *Time on a Curved Line*. They held a meeting in a conference room at the Kyoto Municipal Museum of Art where Nakahara discussed his critical evaluation of the works in the show. I wasn't there, but that was the first time that anybody had critiqued photographic works in Japan. The fact of displaying photographs and of someone discussing their relevance as works of art was pretty rare, so March 1970 was kind of a milestone in this sense, as up until then photographs were just documentary. They were stand-ins for the sculptures that were too big to travel from

Tokyo. So photographs were exhibited just to document the fact that there had been this work of art made.

I exhibited photographs of *Dryice* and *Time on a Curved Line* as works of art in that show. I already had a day job at that time [at a television broadcast company, since April 1969], so I couldn't be present at the exhibition very often. However, everybody was either stepping on the photographs or just walking right by them, and nobody really viewed them as works of art in and of themselves. Other works were receiving attention. One day when I visited a gallery, I was told that Nakahara had said he liked my works, and that was the first time that those photographs saw the light as works of art, by those people present at the critique. I think Nakahara even wrote something about this in a magazine. That May [1970], my photographs were shown in the *Tokyo Biennale* [at the Tokyo Metropolitan Art Museum; it was subtitled *Between Man and Matter* and curated by Nakahara] and were acknowledged as works of art, which was a first in Japan. That's my understanding of how photography entered art. I don't know how much other people would agree with this, but for me, March 1970 and the criticism of Nakahara Yūsuke were very significant.

One of the possibilities I saw in my photographs was that time was recorded in them. Until then, sculpture occupied three-dimensional space, the space we live our lives in. Sculptors have given a lot of thought to the space occupied by sculpture, but we haven't been very good at considering time in this context; it has been ignored. Sculptures have interacted with time in terms of being permanent objects, but nobody has given much thought to time as a changing thing in the context of sculpture. But when I saw the photographs of *Tardiology*, I realized that I could record time as experienced by sculpture. The reason I started photography was because of that. So I set myself apart from other people who began using photography.

McCaffrey: If an American or European artist had made *Tardiology* and watched it disintegrate, they would probably have kept the crumpled cardboard, feeling that "this is my work of art . . . this is something valuable." But in your case, you decided to discard the sculpture's remnants. What philosophical or practical thoughts allowed you to throw them away?

Nomura: Perhaps I should've given it more thought, but it wasn't in any way aesthetically pleasing, and it was really falling apart. It had gotten rained on outside. . . . I don't know, perhaps if I had had some kind of philosophical reason for keeping it, I would've, but I didn't. So there was no philosophy underpinning my decision to throw it away. Maybe it was just a question of space, somewhere to store all that material. At that time, I was in Kyoto, and I had kept the capsules I mentioned before in cardboard boxes for a long time. I had replaced the boxes, of course, and I still have the capsules. But, anyway, I was living in an apartment, and until I could finally afford a warehouse, I had the experience of looking for apartments where I could keep all this stuff, paying a lot of money to moving companies specializing in works of art. I just didn't really have a sense—it didn't occur to me to keep it. That's all. My focus was on the process. I was done with the cardboard. In its place, I had the photographs.

McCaffrey: Tell me about *Dryice* and *Iodine*.

Nomura: *Dryice* and *Iodine* came about because the type of large cardboard sheets needed for *Tardiology* were not commercially available, and I had to make them myself by layering many smaller sheets. It took me many days and a big space to put together the material. After I graduated, I was living and working from my apartment, so I had to come up with sculptures that would allow me to put my ideas into practice without taking up large amounts of space and time. *Dryice* and *Iodine* did not require a lot of preparation, and these works allowed me to record the passage of time and its effect on the mass and form of sculptures.

There are many kinds of matter that change over time. It's more difficult to find some material that does not change. Dry ice and iodine sublimate, which means that the substances do not go through a liquid state—they change directly from the solid state to the gaseous state. This meant that the sculpture wouldn't create a big mess, and it allowed me to limit the type of material that I would use. Instead of just using absolutely anything, I was selecting specific materials for their specific properties. Also, it meant that changes would be more clearly recognizable within a certain amount of time, and I didn't need so much

space or time to prepare the materials, as the sculptural properties I wanted to explore were already present in the raw materials.

McCaffrey: Explain the process of making these works.

Nomura: The process was the same for both. So I'd move the dry ice, weigh the individual blocks, and build the cube. At the end of this series of actions, I'd look at my watch, note the time and total weight, and take a picture. Then I would move on, weigh again, rebuild the cube, look at the watch, write the details down, and take another picture. There was no plan to finish within a certain amount of time, or establish regular intervals between each action. Time was passing as I was working, and the dry ice was disappearing at its own rate, with the weight changing accordingly.

McCaffrey: Did you know about Richard Serra, Gordon Matta-Clark, Robert Smithson, Joseph Beuys, Vito Acconci, or other artists in the late '60s and '70s?

Nomura: When I was making *Tardiology*, *Dryice*, and *Iodine*, I didn't really know much about them, but in May of 1970, Serra and Carl Andre came to Japan because of the *Tokyo Biennale*. I was at the *Paris Biennale* with Gordon Matta-Clark in 1975, and I learned about his work about six months before that. As for Beuys, his work at Documenta had been featured in Japanese magazines prominently, so that's how I found out about him. Vito Acconci wasn't really known in Japan.

McCaffrey: A great deal of the most avant-garde work in Japan emerged from individual artists working under the auspices of a group: Hi Red Center, Gutai, and Mono-ha, to name some of the better-known ones. However, for the most part you worked and continue to work alone. Can you explain why?

Nomura: Well, after I graduated, I had group shows with other people of my age in Kyoto and Osaka. Looking at the history of the exhibits that I'd done at that time, you can see that group shows occurred about once a month, so in that sense, it's not the case that I didn't work with anybody, but nonetheless it wasn't something I necessarily intended.

In terms of proximity, Gutai was in Osaka and therefore close by, and some of the people who had graduated before me had contact with them. I had seen a show of the work of Fontana and Capogrossi at the Gutai Pinacoteca in Osaka [in June 1964], and my impression was basically, "So this is where they have their shows." When I saw their works, I never thought to myself that I would be able to make it as a sculptor if I joined that group. My only thoughts were along the lines of, "Huh, they're doing something different." Artists from Tokyo would come here and have shows as well, but I never really had a reason to tie myself to a larger group.

McCaffrey: What did you know about what would become known as Mono-ha?

Nomura: Sekine Nobuo's *Phase—Mother Earth* was shown in Suma [at the *Biennale of Kobe at Suma Detached Palace Garden: Contemporary Sculpture Exhibition* in October 1968], so I had seen it, but it didn't really impress me. I didn't get as much impact as people say today. And at that time—I was talking about this with someone just the other day—it looked like an *objet*, an interesting shape. It looked to other people like something else, and I don't know why it looked that way to me. That was something I wondered about at the time. But the reason I don't think I was wrong at that time, even today, is because a few years later, Sekine had drilled a large hole into a piece of granite and placed the stone over a pillar, and that was his work of art [*Phase of Nothingness*, 1970, which was shown at the *Venice Biennale*]. When I saw that, my reaction was, "Yeah, that's what I thought. It's an *objet*, nothing more." So the thinking behind his *Phase—Mother Earth* didn't have anything to do with any new concepts; it was just an *objet*, in terms of the idea behind it. That's the only way I've ever been able to view it, from the first time I saw it until now. I want to define art as something beyond merely shape.

Selected Works, 1968–70

Plate 1. *Untitled*, 1968
Transparent plastic capsule, 8 pieces
40¼ x 35½ x 35½ inches (102 x 90 x 90 cm) each

Plate 2. *Tardiology*, 1968–69
Sequence of 8 black-and-white photographs
Left to right: 2 photos, 31½ x 47¼ inches (80 x 120 cm) each (image size); 4 photos, 47¼ x 31½ inches (120 x 80 cm) each (image size); 2 photos, 31½ x 47¼ inches (80 x 120 cm) each (image size)

So I had already received the opinion that sculptures are things that are supposed to stand firm. That was the conceptual framework through which people traditionally viewed sculpture. And my purpose in presenting *Tardiology* was to say, "There's another way."

—Nomura Hitoshi (Interview, p. 8)

Plate 3. Creating *Dryice*, 1969

Plate 4. *Dryice*, Nov. 2, 1969
Sequence of 10 black-and-white photographs
Left to right: 3 photos, 35½ x 23⅝ inches (90 x 59.9 cm) each (image size);
5 photos, 35½ x 26⅜ inches (90 x 67 cm) each (image size); 2 photos,
35½ x 43 inches (90 x 109.1 cm) each (image size)

The fact of displaying photographs and of someone discussing their relevance as works of art was pretty rare, so March 1970 was kind of a milestone in this sense, as up until then photographs were just documentary.

—Nomura Hitoshi (Interview, p. 9)

Plate 5. *Iodine*, March 29, 1970
Sequence of 12 black-and-white photographs
27⅝ x 33⅞ inches (70 x 86 cm) each (image size)

Marking Time

Martha Buskirk

The photographs tell an eloquent story of the structure's collapse. From the very beginning, there are signs of inherent instability, with the weight of the top three rectangular compartments crushing down on a fourth, which bows outward from the pressure. Tenuous-looking dowels appear in the bottom opening, along with guy wires, perhaps slowing its process of folding in upon itself. But the cardboard walls quite evidently cannot support their own weight, since subsequent photos show only two intact rectangles over an increasingly messy layering of compressed material. And then it breaks down completely, into a chaotic pile that demonstrates the force of gravity as final arbitrator.

For Nomura Hitoshi, his 1968–69 *Tardiology* (pl. 2) was both a culmination point and the inauguration of an expanded definition of sculpture that would lead him into linked explorations of photography, sound, and film. Nomura presented the work in front of the Kyoto Municipal Museum of Art in March 1969 as his thesis project, marking the end of his graduate studies. The sculpture curriculum he describes emphasized an exploration of materials and their properties, but one in which stone and wood remained central. His decision to explore something far less stable or historically validated reflected a fortuitous experience outside the classroom.

Nomura was already pushing in new directions with an untitled 1968 work based on multiple plastic spheres that he designed and fabricated (pl. 1). But quite by chance, this early endeavor provided a lesson that took him even further afield. In order to store the work after it returned from exhibition, he fashioned individual cardboard boxes for each component, which he stacked up under his eaves. As he recounts in the interview in this volume, the stacked boxes began to collapse. In contrast to the "beautiful, interesting forms" he was being taught to create as part of his graduate education, the disintegrating cardboard boxes constituted a form that "was 'bad' and caused me a headache, but a form nonetheless."

Once transformed from a problem to a solution, however, the cardboard material also had the potential to redefine the sculptural experience. Rather than presenting an object that

Figure 3. Installation view of *When Attitudes Become Form* at Kunsthalle Bern, March 22–April 27, 1969: Mario Merz, *Acqua Scivola*, and (against wall and on floor) works by Giovanni Anselmo, in Arte Povera Gallery

was completely realized in advance, Nomura consciously courted change, with the work's installation just "the starting point," for a structure where "gravity, the wind, rain, and time" would lead it gradually to fall apart. And because *Tardiology* was designed to be ephemeral, photography became an important part of the process, documenting the temporal demise of the structure and remaining the only permanent record after he discarded the crumpled remains.

Viewed from a Western perspective, the geometry of the initial construction is evocative of minimalism, and Nomura was aware of work by Donald Judd that had been exhibited in Japan in the 1960s. Yet that knowledge seems to have been relatively incidental in comparison to the stack of partially collapsing cardboard storage boxes that provided the direct inspiration for *Tardiology*. Whatever one might speculate about the significance of minimalism for Nomura, his use of cardboard to create a sculptural form designed to fall apart set this pivotal work on a path that led him directly from geometric regularity to an anti-form emphasis on process and materials. In addition, the manner in which he chose to document its mutation aligned his practice with the increasingly central role played by photography in recording and conveying a host of distant or ephemeral manifestations. Although Nomura came to these conclusions independently, there is a striking convergence between his process of discovery, culminating in *Tardiology*'s March 1969 collapse, and a series of international exhibitions over the course of the same year that posited the breakdown of traditional medium divisions, and even distinct movements, in favor of an intersecting series of explorations involving a wide array of materials and processes.

On March 22, 1969, the day after the descent of Nomura's cardboard structure was complete, Harald Szeemann's groundbreaking *When Attitudes Become Form: Works—Concepts—Processes—Situations—Information* opened at the Kunsthalle Bern. International by the standards of the time, the exhibition brought together a range of European and North American works that exceeded any easy attempt at categorization. One of Szeemann's points of departure was Robert Morris's concept of anti form, as articulated in a 1968 essay in *Artforum* and in a closely related show that he organized in Leo Castelli's warehouse space. But Szeemann quickly concluded that Morris's rubric would be too restrictive for an exhibition that he envisioned as cutting across anti form, Arte Povera, conceptual art, and earthworks (to name only the most familiar from a list of relevant trends or movements enumerated by Szeemann, which also included "Micro-emotive Art," "Possible Art," and "Impossible Art").

As the title suggests, Szeemann's emphasis was on shared approach or attitude, rather than perceived unity as a single movement. The art he was after incorporated, among other things, a "shift of interest away from the result towards the artistic process; the use of mundane materials; the interaction of work and material," with the resultant work characterized by "the absolute freedom in the use of materials, as well as the concern for the physical and

chemical properties of the work itself." In contrast to Piet Mondrian or Jackson Pollock, Szeemann argued, who "gave form to their inner bearing, but always in terms of the finished product, the autonomous object," these artists "want the artistic process itself to remain visible in the end product and in the exhibition."[1] And one upshot of the emphasis on process was that, in many cases, rather than transporting objects, Szeemann played host to the artists themselves, who created or completed their work on-site (a familiar gambit in today's biennial culture, but a relatively rare approach to exhibition organization at the time).

Michael Heizer's contribution was perhaps the most invasive, involving the use of a wrecking ball to smash a hole in the cement sidewalk in front of the museum. Both Joseph Beuys and Richard Serra made direct use of the building, Beuys by wedging a line of fat along the base of a wall, and Serra, in another room, by hurling molten lead into the point of intersection between wall and floor. Mario Merz created an elegant but also rough-hewn igloo from sheets of glass, mastic, iron, and a tree limb (fig. 3), while Jannis Kounellis lined a stairwell with bags containing various kinds of grains (fig. 4). Richard Long arrived and then immediately departed on a walk that was represented in the exhibition by a large-type wall text reading, "RICHARD LONG MARCH 19–22 1969 A WALKING TOUR IN THE BERNER OBERLAND"—which meant that he was one among many of the sixty-nine artists in the exhibition checklist represented by information rather than objects.

In Amsterdam, *Op Losse Schroeven: Situaties en Cryptostructuren* piggybacked on Szeemann's exhibition, opening one week before and including many of the same artists so as to consolidate their intercontinental travel. And in New York, the Whitney Museum's *Anti-Illusion: Procedures/Materials*, which opened in May 1969, again emphasized process-based and conceptual works while concentrating on American practitioners (fig. 5). This was also the year that Germano Celant presented an expanded definition of Arte Povera. Stressing the importance of simple materials and processes as well as open-ended experimentation, Celant emphasized in particular the use of animal, vegetable, and mineral elements. In his initial formulation in 1967 exhibitions and publications, Celant focused on how these ideas were being explored in Italy; however, two years later, he expanded his purview to encompass many of the same European and American artists included in Szeemann's exhibition.[2]

For his own part, Nomura's cardboard structure was quickly followed by an exploration of the sculptural possibilities of dry ice as it evaporates. Viewed against the backdrop of work shown in these major exhibitions of 1969, this turn could be articulated as an intersection of the emphasis on process underpinning Morris's anti form and the attraction to materials that

Figure 4. Installation view of *When Attitudes Become Form* at Kunsthalle Bern, March 22–April 27, 1969: Jannis Kounellis, bags of grain in stairwell

embody or conduct energy in the context of Arte Povera. Yet in Nomura's case, the amalgam reflected his specific background, since his turn to sculpture was preceded by an earlier pursuit of science. The properties of dry ice presented a logical outgrowth to the issues explored in *Tardiology*, because the material allowed Nomura to track the passage of time as it correlated to changes in both mass and form.

When *Dryice* (pl. 3) was first exhibited in fall 1969 in the second *Exhibition of Contemporary Plastic Art* in Kamogawa Park, Kyoto, the work involved an element of performance. On five different days during the course of the one-month exhibition, Nomura set up a scenario using blocks of dry ice that were sequentially weighed and then stacked on mats, where he recorded the date, time, and their diminishing mass (pl. 4). Rather than erasing the writing after each weigh-in, he moved the blocks down the mats (corrugated cardboard, rubber, or canvas, on different days), so that the increasing span of written-upon surface corresponded to the diminishing stack of dry ice. If *Tardiology* set Nomura on a trajectory leading to an expanded conception of sculpture, *Dryice* sealed the deal, with a form that literally evaporates as it goes directly from solid to gas, while the work's physical presence is reoriented from substance to photographic documentation. For *Dryice*, process and document are also more closely intertwined than they were for *Tardiology*, with photographs of each stage integrated into the sequential process of weighing, stacking, and writing.

In the immediate aftermath of *Dryice*, Nomura created a strongly linked work, his 1970 *Iodine* (pl. 5), which extended this exploration to another material that changes directly from a solid to a gaseous state. In addition to echoes of the emphasis on basic elements and their properties in the context of Arte Povera, this line of investigation links Nomura to various attempts to join art and science during the 1960s and 1970s—with E.A.T. (Experiments in Art and Technology) being one of the best-known examples of this drive. Yet this connection is perhaps more evident in relation to some of Nomura's recent projects (the solar-paneled car in particular), which require sophisticated engineering, since the early projects emphasized the raw materials themselves for the sculptural properties Nomura identified as inherent to their elemental state.

Of course, growing grass is also a remarkably basic process. Home owners around the world seem to achieve this feat with prosaic regularity. But *Grass Grows* was one of the natural systems that Hans Haacke explored in works from the late 1960s. He also presented gallery and museum goers with water evaporating or chickens hatching and, for *Tokyo Biennale 1970*, water circulating through a network of hoses. The striking thing is not so much the processes themselves but their presentation in an art gallery or museum context, where they disrupt not just art's traditional medium divisions, but broader categories separating art from other disciplines.

Although it does not seem to have reached the stage of serious consideration, Serra made a far more elaborate proposal for *Op Losse Schroeven*. The exhibition catalogue includes Serra's description of a work to be created by heating lead in an airplane at an altitude between fifteen and thirty thousand feet, then dropping it from the plane, with the idea that the liquid lead would harden into a precise spherical mass during its descent (and with the further proviso that it should be dropped over mud or water to prevent the resultant form from shattering).[3] Serra's use of molten lead was destined to remain earthbound, but his interest in pushing materials to their technical limits would find a different outlet in the context of the Art and Technology program initiated by Maurice Tuchman at the Los Angeles County Museum of Art in 1967.

Tuchman's goal was to match artists with specialized expertise by establishing collaborations with industries pursuing advanced production or research, though the result was a decidedly mixed bag, with certain examples of culture clash vividly recounted in the exhibition catalogue / report that eventually resulted.[4] The 1969 pairing between Serra and Kaiser Steel was, however, clearly fortuitous. The resulting *Skullcracker* series, named after the yard where the works were created, involved an overhead magnetic crane, with a skilled operator and several assistants creating (and then disassembling) various stacked arrangements under Serra's direction. The first piece, made of sixteen blocks of cast iron weighing approximately six tons each, was both elegant and breathtaking in the balance maintained by the tilted stack (fig. 6). Other pieces followed, looking far less orderly in the irregular relationship of the individual elements, but all relying on a combination of physical tension, balance, and gravity to maintain their temporary form. Over the course of eight weeks, twenty structures were assembled, photographed, and then taken apart, leaving the photographs as the only enduring evidence of forms that had reverted to raw material.

For Serra, the photographs from the *Skullcracker* series serve a relay function, providing access to works where their transitory existence was inseparable from their intense physicality. In contrast to Nomura's *Tardiology*, they pushed the limits of stability while remaining upright; however, the status of the photographs is similar, remaining as permanent documentation of impermanent sculptural forms. In the interview in this volume, Nomura recalls two experiences: "The actual experience of seeing the work collapse in front of me was satisfying. Then, upon developing the pictures of the process of collapse, I received a second level of satisfaction." But because of the ephemeral nature of that first experience, the work's later audience can only share in the second level of engagement.

Figure 6. Richard Serra, *Stacked Steel Slabs (Skullcracker series)*, 1969. Hot-rolled steel. Overall: 20 x 8 x 10 feet (6.1 x 2.4 x 3.1 m). Installation in Skullcracker Yard, Kaiser Steel Corporation, Fontana, California

The understanding of sculpture in terms of time and space took Nomura in other directions as well, as is evident in his 1970 *Time on a Curved Line* (pl. 6), which presents a photographic record of the artist's progress as he walked along a series of roads for more than seven hours while stopping to document his location at irregular intervals. Here the process is more analogous to the role played by Long in the expanded field mapped by Rosalind Krauss, where "large photographs documenting country hikes" numbered among "rather surprising things that have come to be called sculpture," part of a list that in turn precipitated her understanding of sculpture as one term within an array that also encompasses marked sites and site constructions.[5]

The photographs were central to Nomura's early reception. Significantly, the next time he showed the work involving dry ice, it was photographs from the earlier exhibition, now titled *Dryice 1969*, which appeared together with *Time on a Curved Line* in the 1970 *Kyoto Independent Exhibition*—where attention from the critic Nakahara Yūsuke led to further exhibitions and validation of the photographs as art.[6] In short order, Nomura's work was also included in *Tokyo Biennale 1970—Between Man and Matter*, with its cross section of international art heavily oriented toward conceptual practices. It is also interesting to note that at *Tokyo Biennale 1970*, Nomura exhibited yet another version of the dry-ice procedure. *Dryice 1970* appears in lists of Nomura's works as photographs only—indicating that the evaporation scenario he set up on March 28 of that year was not generated for an exhibition, but existed purely to be used as the basis for a series of images. And that photo sequence is more formally consistent. Rather than moving the camera around, closer and farther away in relation to the evaporating ice, he has maintained it in a fixed position to record a process of disappearance that therefore takes place along two axes, with the dry-ice blocks diminishing through evaporation, but also through distance, as they are placed progressively farther from the stationary camera. *Iodine*, created one day later, on March 29, is similar in two respects: it involves another substance that moves directly from solid to gas, and it was created in private, rather than for the context of an exhibition (with the photographic work that resulted exhibited in quick succession at a 1970 solo show at Galerie 16 and then at *Tokyo Biennale 1970*).

The turn toward photography is consistent with simultaneous developments in European and American art during the 1960s and 1970s, in which there is a strong emphasis on the photograph as document, often reflecting a casual, snapshot approach decidedly at odds with the formal rigor associated with art photography. The photographic document (sometimes complemented by film or video) quickly became the relay for a whole host of remote or ephemeral forms, with de-aestheticized versions of photography facilitating the transmission of a wide variety of phenomena, from earthworks to performances, and also figuring in overlaps between art and archival practices. Early evidence of the back-and-forth movement between sculpture and photography is provided by the appearance of Robert Smithson's *Spiral Jetty* in the 1970 exhibition *Information* at the Museum of Modern Art (MoMA) in New York, where photographs of the work demonstrated the importance of such documents for conveying information about distant or fleeting manifestations (fig. 7).

Even though the path forged by Nomura was founded on his own amalgam of art and science, his early works can readily be understood in relation to the far-flung series of experiments that have been loosely grouped together under the rubric of global conceptual art.[7] But

what to make of the parallels? Can they be described as a shared tendency, or is it a far more amorphous convergence, based on largely unrelated responses to historical forces that are at once globally interconnected and locally specific?

There are, for example, some rather remarkable correspondences between Nomura's and Vito Acconci's early photo-based work, even though there seems to have been no familiarity in either direction. At about the same time that Nomura was incorporating photographic documentation into his process of recording the evaporation of dry ice, Acconci was including the act of taking the photograph in a number of his works, not as a secondary document, but as integral to the process. One sees this interconnection in Acconci's 1969 *Coming to Rest*, which was based on the activity (defined according to text contained within the work) of "throwing a ball out on the ground in front of me, & snapping photographs until the ball comes to a stop." Four black-and-white snapshots show a barely discernable ball receding into the distance on a nondescript sidewalk, with the action indicated by the text next to each image: "Drop—roll—look—click—" next to the first, then "roll—look—click—," "roll—look—click," and "roll—look—click—stop—" alongside the last photo. Even more suggestive is Acconci's 1969 *Stretch* (fig. 8), from a series of early works he categorized as "Moving My Body into Place," which consists of four haphazardly framed photographs taken in Central Park that were produced, according to the accompanying text, "Stretching as far as I can over my head, out to my left, down to my feet, out to my right; taking a photograph from each position."[8] Other works in the series involved his taking a photo each time he blinked, or falling forward and taking a photo as he hit the ground.

Nomura began a similar series of explorations with his 1970 *Jump*, taking a succession of photographs while jumping up and down holding a camera. His 1972 *Turning the Arm with a Movie Camera: Person, Landscape* (pl. 8) operates with a similar idea, as the camera becomes an extension of the body rather than of sight. The 1972 work involves a double perspective: there is the landscape captured by the movie camera in Nomura's hands, but also a second camera captures Nomura's bodily movement. In the film version of the work, the

Figure 8. Vito Acconci, *Stretch*, 1969. Gelatin silver prints, chalkboard spray paint, chalk, and marker on foam core. 54 x 54 inches (137.2 x 137.2 cm). Museum of Contemporary Art, Chicago, Gerald S. Elliott Collection

vantage points are interspersed, cutting from footage showing Nomura holding the camera to what the moving camera has captured. Photographic versions present sequences of images, both person and landscape. A related work, his 1972 *Center of Gravity: Movement* (pl. 9), strips the action down to the body alone, leaning and then falling forward, but without the more unexpected inclusion of the camera perspective tracing the action from within.

The amount of information contained within the photographs themselves, either individually or in sequence, is, however, an important distinction. Acconci's photographs truly were snapshots (with the camera used for *Coming to Rest* specified by the text within the work as an amateur-style Kodak Instamatic 124). In Nomura's case, the apparent simplicity of means belies a concern with how much the photograph can contain as well as convey. And bringing a camera into a situation alters its dynamics, as Nomura evidently recognized from early on.

That tension is particularly evident in Nomura's 1970 *Time on a Curved Line*. We know from the text within the photos what day the stroll took place, and we can figure out how long it took. For more than seven hours, Nomura walked along, documenting his progress in the series of photographs that constitutes the work. Either the roads he followed were notable for a near-total absence of almost any sort of distinguishing landmark or Nomura studiously avoided such features. His route apparently traversed a landscape that changed very little, over many miles, or Nomura walked extremely slowly. In some of the photographs, a car appears— but never more than one, so it seems that he wisely chose a lightly traveled region for a project that involved crouching in the middle of the street to make chalk notations. And in just a couple of the images, where he has stood somewhat closer to the lettering to take the photo, a partial silhouette of the artist presents a fleeting trace of his presence behind the camera.

The evidence of the work itself indicates that Nomura did more than just walk: clearly he walked and photographed. In addition, before taking each photograph, he paused long enough to write the date and time on the road, in large chalk lettering that is the central focus of each image. So, at the very least, he walked, stopped at somewhat irregular intervals, noted the time, transcribed the date and time onto the roadway, stepped back from the lettering to take a picture, and then recommenced his walking. The work is therefore about duration, but also delay, in various ways. For its audience, the specific date, February 22, 1970, places the sequence clearly in the past. There would also have been a lag between his taking the photographs and getting the film processed, so Nomura himself saw the images only after the fact. And within the act itself, the moment was already slipping away. Even if Nomura moved at an extremely frenetic pace, it is difficult to imagine that he could have gone from noting the time, writing it in large, steady lettering on the road, and moving back to take the picture in less than a minute. Therefore, the initial act of taking the photo already incorporated a gap in relation to the time notations thus documented.

Had Nomura's early work been more visible in the West, this investigation of the role of the document would have fit quite nicely into a number of major 1970 exhibitions of conceptual art, particularly MoMA's *Information*. Nomura does make a passing appearance in Lucy Lippard's *Six Years: The Dematerialization of the Art Object from 1966 to 1972*, in the entry for *Tokyo Biennale 1970*, but he could certainly have played a more central role in her cross section of developments.[9] Intriguing comparisons, among the examples cited by Lippard, include Hanne Darboven's obsessive numerical calculations tracing the passage of time; excerpts from Douglas Huebler's series of duration and location works; Robert Barry's release of different forms of inert gas (documented in photographs that record only the open containers from which helium, neon, argon, krypton, and xenon gases are presumably escaping); On Kawara's *I met, I went*, and *I got up* series based on cryptic notations recording the artist's passage through time and place; Ed Ruscha's *Every Building on the Sunset Strip* (fig. 9); and a work by Jan Dibbets, described by the artist as a sculpture, that used photos and diagrams to trace the territory of a robin while also attempting to alter its behavior through the introduction of perching poles. Barry's subtitle for his gas pieces, "from a measured volume to an infinite expansion," is particularly suggestive in relation to the themes traced by Nomura, as is another 1969 work, Barry's purely text-based statement: "All of the things I know but of which I am not at the moment thinking—1:36 P.M.; 15 June 1969, New York."

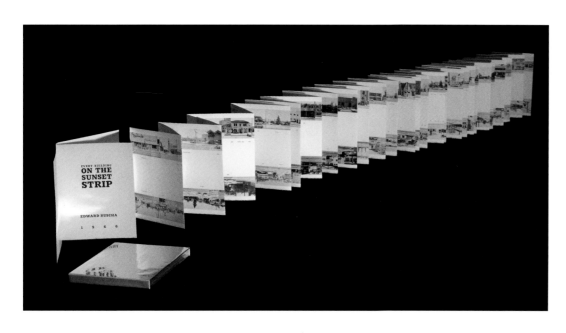

Figure 9. Ed Ruscha, *Every Building on the Sunset Strip*,
1966. Photographic book, black offset paper, folded
and glued. 7⅛ x 5⅝ x ⅜ inches (18.1 x 14.3 x 0.9 cm)
(closed dimensions)

"All" or "every" inevitably describes a tall order. Ruscha pulled it off in his 1966 *Every Building on the Sunset Strip*, with the first word of the title describing an ambitious agenda realized through a carefully structured shooting plan that yielded an accordion-style book, 299½ inches long when fully extended, presenting buildings arranged along the top and bottom of the page in a layout that corresponds to the two sides of the street. Martha Rosler took the opposite tack, with her 1974/75 *The Bowery in Two Inadequate Descriptive Systems*, presenting unpopulated black-and-white photographs of the locale juxtaposed with an amazingly colorful compendium of words and phrases related to drinking and drunks—with their conjunction making the point that neither of these, taken separately or together, is capable of conveying the full dynamics of the down-and-out neighborhood.

In a series of works created between 1970 and 1975, Nomura investigated the interplay between sight and sound, exploring both photography and language as the basis for recording and describing. For *Telephone Eyeshot I* and *II* (pls. 21, 22), recorded on July 6, 1970, Nomura entered a series of phone booths between his home and the Kyoto National Museum of Modern Art and, after using a compass to determine due north, proceeded to recount everything that he was seeing in that one direction, while a collaborator at the museum recorded the reports at the other end of the line.[10] The sets of descriptions, totaling 15 minutes, 37 seconds for the first and 13 minutes, 21 seconds for the second, were then cut as phonograph records that were presented in conjunction with photographs shot in the same direction. Thus, two analog methods were combined, to create a convergence of photographs and verbal accounts that are both full and inherently insufficient.

The series continued with various other verbal records, including the process of Nomura making various purchases, going to a jazz café, or reading poetry against various background sounds (pls. 17, 19, 20, 23, 24). For one in particular, the May 17, 1974, phonograph record that incorporates *Bank* (10 minutes, 20 seconds) and *Disc Cutting* (12 minutes, 30 seconds), the process turns in upon itself, since the two conversations concern sending payment for record plates and arranging with an engineer to have them cut (pl. 18). There is a distant echo of Morris's 1961 *Box with the Sound of Its Own Making*, in which Morris both amplified and subverted the modernist idea of medium specificity and self-referentiality by presenting a small walnut box that hides within itself a speaker and a three-and-one-half-hour recorded tape set up to play back all of the sounds associated with the process of constructing the box. But where Morris set up a closed circle, Nomura's conversations about the logistics of creating the work are simultaneously self-contained and obviously fragmentary, suggesting the multiple dimensions intrinsic to any given situation or process.

The daunting challenge of "every" is even more apparent in Nomura's *Ten-Year Photobook or The Brownian Motion of Eyesight* (pls. 10–13), an extended project undertaken between 1972 and 1982 that was based on his ambitious attempt to photograph everything he saw. There was also the equally hard-to-grasp quality of randomness, indicated by the project's subtitle, which refers to botanist Robert Brown's 1827 observation regarding the motion of pollen grains suspended in water. For Nomura, there was an equivalent between the way someone's gaze will traverse a scene, in seemingly haphazard fashion, and random movement taking place on a particulate level.

Shooting a hundred feet of film each month, Nomura produced thousands of individual images, often in short sequences that exploited the capacity of his classic 16mm Bolex to shoot in brief bursts and at variable rates of speed.[11] The result is an immense compendium of individual images. In one version of the work, the individual frames are reproduced in books with twenty-one photos per page, one book per month, for each of the 120 months of the project. In another version, the images are presented via video, four frames per second. Thus, Nomura used his movie camera in hybrid fashion, somewhere between motion-picture and still-image production, in a manner that to a certain extent reverses a key development in the twentieth-century history of photography, when the highly portable Leica camera was created using redeployed 35mm movie stock. The work also points to the significance of time as the basis for distinguishing between these two mediums, since the thousands of still photographs that resulted from Nomura's hybrid process would have amounted to less than three minutes of film per month had he been shooting continuously at a normal rate of twenty-four frames per second.

The goal of recording everything is clearly bound to fail, as is the idea that the camera might provide a direct equivalent to sight (limitations that contributed to Nomura's decision to bring the project to an end).[12] We don't see photographically, even if photographs do help extend vision and also serve as memory aids that can, in time, supplant more inchoate impressions. Nor is sight equivalent to how a movie camera records, as is evident when faced with the tedium of real-time documentation or the nausea-inducing movement of hand-held camera footage.

But for Nomura, the camera is not simply an extension of sight. It is also about time, as expressed in sequences of images tracing changing matter, or in records that reflect the body's movement through space. And Nomura seems to have embraced the infinite regress that puts the project of recording every experience firmly beyond our grasp. As part of his *Ten-Year Photobook*, Nomura turned his camera upward, toward the sun and moon—indeed, the entire cosmos—setting the stage for a whole new series of investigations that would carry on the play between the specific and infinite already implied by his early explorations of time, space, and matter.

Notes

1. Harald Szeemann, "Zur Ausstellung," in *When Attitudes Become Form: Works—Concepts—Processes—Situations—Information* (Bern: Kunsthalle Bern, 1969), n.p. For the English translation of this introduction (as well as other background information about the exhibition), see Harald Szeemann, *With by through because towards despite: Catalogue of All Exhibitions 1957–2005*, ed. Tobia Bezzola and Roman Kurzmeyer (Zürich: Edition Voldemeer; Vienna and New York: Springer, 2007), 225–61.

2. See Germano Celant, *Art Povera* (New York: Praeger, 1969), particularly 225–30. This English-language publication is a translation of the 1969 exhibition catalogue published by Gabriele Mazzotta Publishers, Milan.

3. See the second (foldout) section of artists' proposals in *Op Losse Schroeven: Situaties en Cryptostructuren* (Amsterdam: Stedelijk Museum, 1969), n.p.

4. See Maurice Tuchman, *A Report on the Art and Technology Program of the Los Angeles County Museum of Art, 1967–1971* (Los Angeles: Los Angeles County Museum of Art, 1971).

5. Rosalind Krauss, "Sculpture in the Expanded Field" (1978), reprinted in *The Originality of the Avant-Garde and Other Modernist Myths* (Cambridge, Mass.: MIT Press, 1985), 276–90.

6. On Nakahara Yūsuke's critical validation, see Nomura's interview in this volume. It is also interesting to note that both Carl Andre and Sol LeWitt, who were in Japan in conjunction with *Tokyo Biennale 1970*, visited Nomura's 1970 exhibition at Galerie 16 in Kyoto, where they had an opportunity to interact with Nomura. See *Nomura Hitoshi—Genesis of Life: The Universe, the Sun, DNA* (Mito: Contemporary Art Center, 2000), Appendix (Chronology), 3.

7. Global versions of conceptual art were traced in the exhibition *Global Conceptualism: Points of Origin, 1950s–1980s*, curated by Luis Camnitzer, Jane Farver, and Rachel Weiss. Nomura figures in the chapter by Reiko Tomii (in cooperation with Chiba Shigeo), "Concerning the Institution of Art: Conceptualism in Japan," in *Global Conceptualism: Points of Origin, 1950s–1980s* (New York: Queens Museum, 1999), 15–29.

8. Reproduced in the context of a special issue on Vito Acconci, *Avalanche* 6 (Fall 1972): 6.

9. Lucy Lippard, *Six Years: The Dematerialization of the Art Object from 1966 to 1972* (1973; repr., Berkeley and Los Angeles: University of California Press, 1997), 165.

10. Iwaki Ken'ichi, "*Tardiology* and *HEARING*: On Hitoshi Nomura's Early Works," in *Seeing: Contingency and Necessity; The Work of Hitoshi Nomura* (Kyoto: Akaaka Art Publishing, 2006), 40.

11. One description of *Ten-Year Photobook* indicates that Nomura shot 100 feet, or 4,300 frames, per month—an inconsistency, given that 16mm film has 40 frames per foot. Iwaki, *Seeing: Contingency and Necessity*, 21.

12. See Nomura's discussion of the project in Iwaki, *Seeing: Contingency and Necessity*, 19 and 21.

Selected Works, 1970–93

Plate 6. *Time on a Curved Line*, Feb. 22, 1970
Black-and-white photograph
35½ x 35½ inches (90 x 90 cm) (image size)

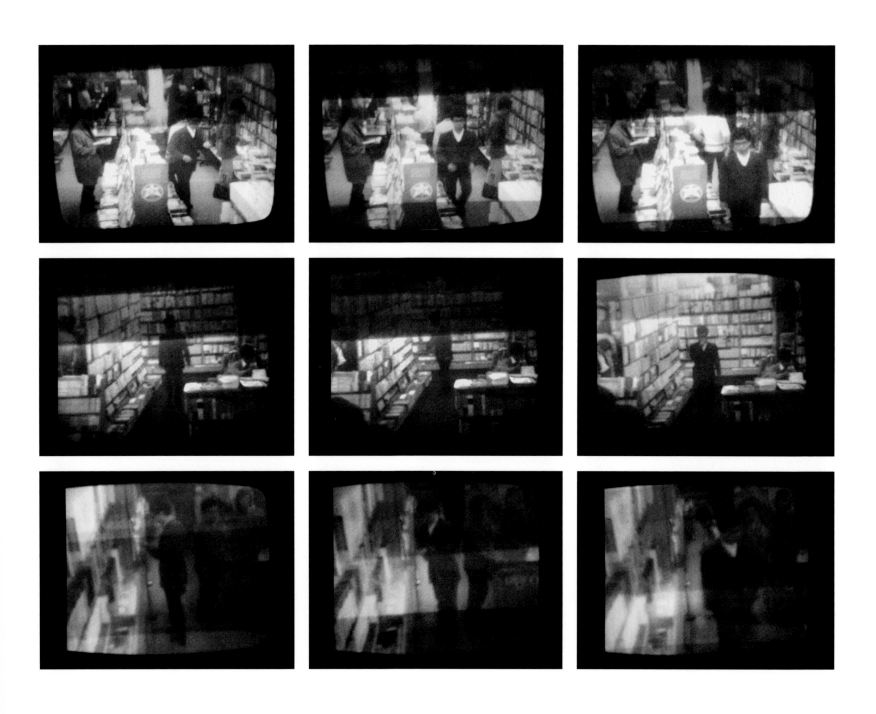

Plate 7. *'N' on TV in a Bookshop for 10 Minutes Everyday* (film stills), 1971
Nov. 11–19, 1971
16mm film, black and white, 6 min.

Plate 8. *Turning the Arm with a Movie Camera: Person, Landscape* (film stills), 1972
Jan. 14, 1972
16mm film, black and white, 11 min.

Plate 9. *The Center of Gravity: Movement* (film stills), 1972
Jan. 26, 1972
16mm film, black and white, 5 min.

When a person looks at a scene, he/she may look at the whole scene, or may focus on a particular segment. But either way, his/her eye will seemingly move around at random. They even resemble the Brownian movement of minute particles.

—Nomura Hitoshi, quoted in *Seeing: Contingency and Necessity; The Work of Hitoshi Nomura*, by Iwaki Ken'ichi (Kyoto: Akaaka Art Publishing, 2006), 18

Plate 10. *The Brownian Motion of Eyesight* (film still), 1972–73
16mm film, black and white, 4 frames per second, 5 hours

Plate 11. *The Brownian Motion of Eyesight* (film stills), 1972–73

Plate 12. Installation view of *Ten-Year Photobook or The Brownian Motion of Eyesight*, 1972–82, at Toyota Municipal Museum of Art, 2001
120 photobooks
10⅜ x 9⅛ x 1¾ inches (26.2 x 23 x 4.2 cm) each

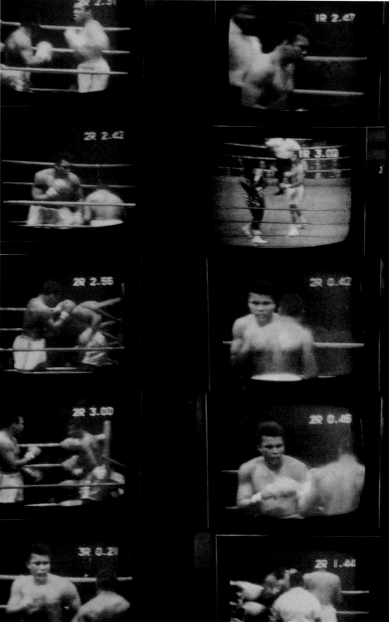

Plate 13. *Ten-Year Photobook or The Brownian Motion of Eyesight* (detail), 1972–82

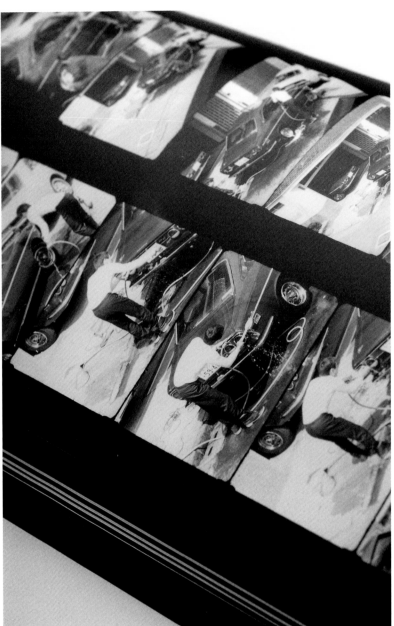

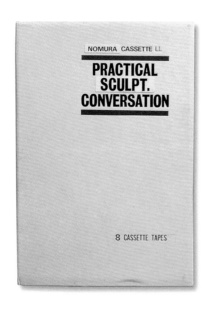

Plate 14. *Practical Sculpt. Conversation*, 1970–74
Tape for listening-comprehension exercises. Later made into record and transcript.

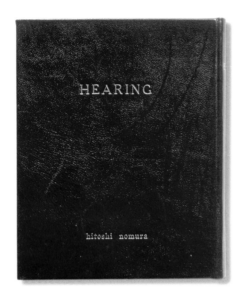

Plate 15. *Hearing*, 1975
A collection of all of *Hearing* under one cover

Plate 16. *A Special Room for Hearing*, 1970–76

Plate 17. *Big Beat*, Feb. 9, 1974, 12 min., 55 sec.
Big Beat, Feb. 9, 1974, 12 min., 35 sec.
Going to Big Beat Jazz Café.
Sounds of municipal streetcar and city,
and jazz music.

Plate 18. *Bank*, May 17, 1974, 10 min., 20 sec.
Disc Cutting, May 17, 1974, 12 min., 30 sec.
Sending payment for an order of record plates
for 6 discs. Ordering cutting from engineer.
The sounds of these conversations.

Plate 19. *Drain Pipe*, Dec. 16, 1972,
12 min., 30 sec.
D.X. Antenna, Dec. 16, 1972, 7 min., 30 sec.
Going to buy a washing machine drain hose
and a TV antenna. Conversation with shop
worker and situational sounds.

Plate 20. *Vinyl*, Aug. 2, 1972, 6 min., 25 sec.
Packing Tape, Aug. 2, 1972, 6 min., 00 sec.
Conversation while buying plastic sheeting
for covering eight 1.3-meter cardboard
boxes and tape for taping it down, and
situational sounds.

Plate 21. *Telephone Eyeshot I*, July 6, 1970,
15 min., 37 sec.
Using a telephone booth, ascertain north via a
compass magnet and report everything that can
be seen in that direction to 075-761-4113.

Plate 22. *Telephone Eyeshot II*, July 6, 1970,
13 min., 21 sec.
Continued from *Telephone Eyeshot I*. Reports
from eight telephone booths in total, each report
three minutes long (due to call time limits in
effect at the time).

Plate 23. *Vocal Chords*, Feb. 20, 1975,
9 min., 59 sec.
Vocal Chords, Feb. 20, 1975, 9 min., 29 sec.
With environmental sounds of city streets
(helicopter sounds, etc.) and machine noises,
reading aloud the final syllables of poems
by Nakae Toshio.

Plate 24. *Words Rain*, Nov. 4, 1974,
12 min., 11 sec.
Sheep, Nov. 4, 1974, 13 min., 18 sec.
With rain sounds and the baaing of sheep,
reading aloud the final syllables of haiku
by Ozaki Hōsai and Taneda Santoka.

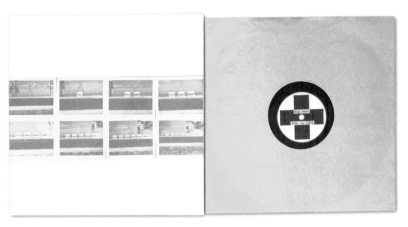

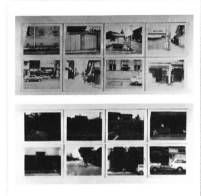

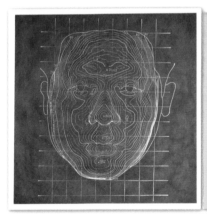

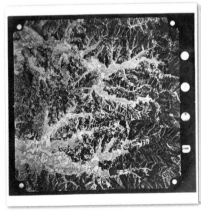

Plate 25. Installation view of *Liquid Nitrogen: −196° C*, 1971

Plate 26. Installation view of *Liquid Nitrogen: −196° C*, 1971
March 20, 1971
Liquid nitrogen, cardboard
10 sheets, 15¾ x 10⅞ inches (40 x 27.5 cm) each

Plate 27. Installation view of *Time Arrow: Oxygen −183° C*, 1993,
at Toyota Municipal Museum of Art, 2001
Liquid oxygen, 6 Dewar flasks
H. 19¾ x diam. 8¼ inches (50 x 21 cm) each

Plate 28. *Time Arrow: Oxygen −183° C* (detail), 1993

The Culture of Showing:
The Operational Context for
Nomura Hitoshi's Early Works

Reiko Tomii

In 1968–69, when Nomura Hitoshi conceived *Tardiology* (pl. 2) for his master's thesis project and presented it in front of the Kyoto Municipal Museum of Art, he made a breakthrough at once in his own art practice, in the evolution of Non-Art (*Hi-geijutsu*) in Japan, and in the global history of art of the 1960s.

Tardiology was a breakthrough in his own early oeuvre because it opened up new possibilities for sculpture through his affinity for raw and fugitive materiality (it was made of cheap cardboard sheets), his focus on the process rather than on the final form (he wanted to create a collapsing structure), and his use of photography (he shot the entire process rather than leaving the task to a photographer). In brief, he was beginning to devise ways to "sculpt time."[1] This would soon lead to a series of photo- and film-based explorations, including *Dryice* (1969–70) (pl. 4) and *Iodine* (1970) (pl. 5), and would be developed into *'moon' score* (1975–ongoing), the pivotal series that in turn opened a door for him to engage the entire macro- and microcosm in his work.

With *Tardiology*, Nomura marked a new stage in the evolution of Non-Art in 1960s Japan by reclaiming a commitment to materiality, which the preceding Anti-Art (*Han-geijutsu*) generation had either sensationalized by its chaotic embrace of *objets* (junk objects),[2] negated through its subversive deployment of performances, or undermined in its nascent conceptualism. He instead introduced a methodical approach to his investigation of formless forms. This seemingly puts him in the same faction as Mono-ha (Things School), a Tokyo-based movement known for installations that intensely emphasized raw materiality and the physicality of matter (*busshitsu*). However, Nomura set himself apart from Mono-ha with his singular innovation: solving the conundrum of art and photography that haunted many Anti-Art performances, by unifying the two acts (art-making and photographing) within a single work. He thus became the first Japanese artist to employ photography as a primary expressive medium in the context of art.

The characteristics of *Tardiology* as outlined above make Nomura, like many other Anti-Art and Non-Art practitioners, a convergence point of the concurrently developing global

OPPOSITE: Figure 10. *Dryice*, Oct. 19, 1969. Dry ice, corrugated cardboard. 120 sheets, 82¾ x 98½ inches (210 x 250 cm) each

and local narratives. Indeed, the international contemporaneity in contemporary art practices was already recognized at the time, especially when the critic Nakahara Yūsuke curated the legendary *Tokyo Biennale 1970* and gathered together forty artists from around the world who shared the general tendencies of Postminimalism, conceptualism, and Arte Povera. At its venue, the Tokyo Metropolitan Art Museum, Nomura's photographic *Dryice*, as well as the works by such Japanese artists as Enokura Kōji, Horikawa Michio, Matsuzawa Yutaka, and Narita Katsuhiko, occupied the same space as those by Carl Andre, Daniel Buren, Christo, Luciano Fabro, Jannis Kounellis, and Richard Serra, among others.

A seminal moment of postwar art history on a global scale, the period around 1970 still requires concerted, in-depth studies. Especially important is a comparative study that will allow us to see "similar yet dissimilar" characteristics of each practice within a larger reservoir of resonances and connections—a task that demands localized knowledge to properly contextualize a given artist's work.[3] In light of his significant contribution, Nomura offers a pertinent starting point in expanding our localized understanding of the art of the late 1960s and early 1970s. Since Nomura himself explains the internal logic of his evolution elsewhere in this publication, this essay will focus on the external aspects that influenced his evolution, although he might not have been conscious of them (in fact, he confesses, in the interview in this volume, that he was not). The external and practical environment is as defining an element in any artist's operation as his internal logic is. This is particularly true in the case of 1960s Japan, as the sites for vanguard practices were rapidly expanding throughout the decade, and practitioners were increasingly gaining legitimacy in the official art world. In this development, Nomura both affected and was affected by the change.

1960s Art in Japan and the Culture of Showing

A few factors complicate our study of international contemporaneity circa 1970, making it difficult to seamlessly merge the global and local narratives.

One is the sophisticated art-critical discourse of 1960s Japan, which reflected and responded to a different modernity that had arisen and developed on this Asian archipelago. The practice and the discourse evolved in tandem, feeding off each other, to shape *gendai bijutsu*, or "contemporary art," the rubric under which vanguard practices came to be recognized in the official art world.[4] Chief critics were the Big Three (Haryū Ichirō, Nakahara Yūsuke, and Tōno Yoshiaki), who began their work in the 1950s. They were followed in the 1960s, among others, by critics Miyakawa Atsushi and Ishiko Junzō and artist-ideologues Hikosaka Naoyoshi, Lee Ufan, and Yasunao Tone, who all contributed to building the *gendai* ("contemporary") discourse.[5]

Another reason lies in the artist's operational environments in Japan that markedly differed from those in Europe and America, which, like it or not, serves as the primary point of reference for the globalized perspective. Granted, the resonances of practice observed at *Tokyo Biennale 1970*, for example, were characterized by the shared spirit of "conceptualism" and "dematerialization." Yet the Japanese and Euro-American artists arrived at their respective solutions from different motivations and through different paths. (By "conceptualism" and "dematerialization," I mean the strategic reevaluations of art-making; whereas the former emphasized the conceptual processes and often involved the institutional critique, the latter varyingly focused on form-making and stripped the privileged auras of "painting" and "sculpture" as such from the work.)

A major difference lay in the extent to which the art market and patronage benefited contemporary artists in respective locales, in particular a disparity between Japan and New York. Japan's—and, in fact, Tokyo's—cadre of commercial dealers specializing in contemporary art was limited to just three (Tokyo, Minami, and Nantenshi Gallery), which tended to prioritize such prewar modernists as Saitō Yoshishige and only slowly, by late in the decade, began to show younger artists such as Takamatsu Jirō and Sekine Nobuo, to name just two major figures from two different generations. In the case of Nomura, having made an auspicious start by being included in *Tokyo Biennale 1970*, he had to make his living by working full time for the art department of a television network until he began teaching at his alma mater, Kyoto City University of Arts (Kyoto Shiritsu Geijutsu Daigaku), in 1988.

In contrast, New York boasted a group of contemporary art galleries. Not only did they deal in the cutting-edge artists, enjoying a substantially larger set of collectors hungrier for new art than in Tokyo; but they also actively supported their artists, even when they saw little immediate commercial gain. Virginia Dwan's financial backing for such market-defying Earthworks masterpieces as *Double Negative* and *Spiral Jetty* was phenomenal; so was Leo Castelli's aid to Richard Serra and others, by providing stipends with few strings attached. The complex and nuanced situation makes it difficult to discuss the often-mentioned "commodification" and ensuing "dematerialization" of artwork in any simplistic terms. To say the least, however, the *perception* of "financial support," whether of commodified kinds or not, through the forces of market and patronage, undeniably did exist there.

If the situation in New York allowed a general assumption of salability and collectability for contemporary artworks, circumstances in Japan engendered a contrary expectation, that contemporary art would never sell. The attitude of artists in each locale to their respective situation could not have been more divergent. American artists could not be indifferent to the growing commercialism there, with some progressive practitioners devising strategies to subvert it; Japanese vanguardists mostly operated outside financial concerns, preoccupied with making and, more important, showing their works but paying little heed to the future of their art.

Significantly, this Japanese attitude translated into what I call a "culture of showing," wherein showing took far greater precedence over everything else. Granted, "showing" is an indispensable component in the visual artist's operation outside his or her studio, even before the consideration of "selling" enters the equation, if at all. However, in the culture of showing of 1960s Japan, the utter unlikelihood of sales drove showing to become the end itself, whether that meant exhibiting object-based works or presenting ephemeral or object-less works. The latter were typically conceptualist or performative and customarily shown outside the conventional exhibition venues.

Symptoms of the Culture of Showing

Symptoms of the culture of showing abound in Japanese art in the 1960s, which in art-historical terms actually spans the period from 1954 to 1974, encompassing Gutai, Anti-Art, and Non-Art.[6] In fact, the whole trajectory of this expanded 1960s demonstrates the central place that "showing" occupied. The most spectacular instances are performative works, in which "making" and "showing" were more or less equated. Gutai's innovative "onstage" exhibitions, as well as the members' famed "actions" taken in front of the press, left a rich legacy to explore.[7] A poster child for Anti-Art, Ushio Shinohara invented many outrageous works and acts specifically to court publicity in the popular media as his "reward,"[8] and his *Boxing Painting* was enshrined by the American photographer William Klein in his photobook *Tokyo* (1964).[9] While Hi Red Center specialized in creating clandestine events in the public sphere,[10] Zero Dimension (Zero Jigen) staged naked rituals (*gishiki*) on the streets, receiving plenty of publicity.[11] In Non-Art, the site of operation was extended into landscapes, as Group "I" created *Hole* (1965) on the bank of the Nagara River in central Japan (fig. 11), The Play began its voyage into landscape by staging *Voyage: A Happening in an Egg* (1968) on the Pacific Ocean (fig. 15), and GUN performed *Event to Change the Image of Snow* (1970) on the bank of the Shinano River.[12]

"Works had short lives back then":[13] a less glamorous symptom was thus saliently described by Akasegawa Genpei, a central figure of Anti-Art. The works were short-lived because "Nobody thought of preserving their works at that time,"[14] recalled Kaidō Hideo, a cultural reporter for the Yomiuri Newspaper Company who was instrumental in organizing his employer's independent exhibition (*Yomiuri Independent Exhibition*), which became a major breeding ground of Anti-Art. The priority placed on showing was exemplified by the participating artists' frequent requests to the organizers to "destroy, discard, or sell [the exhibited works] to a junk collector." As Akasegawa pointed out, many artists' meager economic circumstances made it impossible for them to keep their works, even if they wanted. They generally lacked space to store their works; and what little they managed to store could have been discarded or lost when they needed more room for life's essentials or they moved.[15]

The practically nonexistent market must have exacerbated the situation. Still, the artists appear to have been unconcerned about the paucity of sales opportunities. For example, Gutai artists never thought that anybody would want to buy their works—that is, before they met Michel Tapié, a French dealer-critic, who promoted (in other words, marketed) their works outside Japan. Until then, Shiraga Kazuo, known for his foot painting, seldom doubted the legitimacy of paper as his painting support; it was inexpensive, especially when he had to create large-scale works, such as those he showed at the *1st* and *2nd Gutai Exhibitions*, the largest being 800 centimeters, or 26 feet, wide.[16] It was Tapié who told Shiraga and other Gutai artists to paint on canvas, because canvases were easier to transport and, more important, commanded higher prices.

Therefore, it is no surprise that Nomura did not consider preserving his cardboards, as indifference to preservation was the norm, rather than an exception, in the culture of showing. Besides, the point of *Tardiology* centered on the process, not on the final product. Still, Nomura's attitude makes a striking comparison with such process-oriented works as Richard Serra's

Cutting Device: Base Plate Measure of the same year, which entered the collection of the Museum of Modern Art, New York, in 1979. From the Japanese standard, it would have been unimaginable to save lumber and metal plates, let alone think about these materials constituting a collectible work. (A Japanese artist could have recycled these "relics" as building materials, just as Koshimizu Susumu did with fifteen incised wood planks of his Mono-ha masterwork *From Surface to Surface* in 1971; the work was later reconstructed, in 1994.) As far as Nomura was concerned, what mattered to him was the preservation of the process via photography. Yet photography had a vexing place in the culture of showing.

The Place of Photography in the Culture of Showing

At first glance, photography seems an ideal tool of preservation in the culture of showing. A variety of ephemeral works were photographically documented, ranging from Gutai's outdoor and performative works to Hi Red Center's iconic *Cleaning Event* (1964) (fig. 13), from Group "I"'s hole-digging to GUN's dynamic snow painting. The importance of such documentation cannot be emphasized enough. No matter how inventive or radical a work might have been, if it was not visually documented, it is not easy to maintain the memory of it in art history. One such case is a hole-digging Happening of Miyazaki Junnosuke, a member of Kyūshū-ha (Kyūshū School), who tacitly dug six or seven square holes, each about six feet deep, on the beach of Fukuoka on the occasion of the collective's overnight performance-party entitled *Grand Gathering of Heroes* in 1962.[17] Needless to say, Miyazaki's hole-digging, along with that of Group "I" and Gutai's Yoshihara Michio (1956), set historical precedents for the

Figure 11. Group "I," *Hole*, 1965. Documentary photograph of performance at *Gifu Independent Art Festival*

73

Figure 12. Sekine Nobuo, *Phase—Mother Earth*, 1968. Documentary photograph of site-specific sculpture at Suma Detached Palace Garden

hole-digging of Sekine Nobuo's *Phase—Mother Earth* (1968), which jump-started the Mono-ha movement (fig. 12).

It was most often the case that photographers other than the artists themselves shot performance works, and the resulting documentary photographs customarily remained under the control of the photographer, who then marketed them to the print media, which in turn helped generate publicity for the artists. It should be noted that these photographers, such as Hirata Minoru and Ōtsuji Seiji, almost never kept the original prints. The concept of "original prints" as display objects—let alone "vintage prints" as marketable commodity—did not catch on in Japan until well into the 1980s. For example, the revered photographer Kimura Ihei considered that the true form of photography might be achieved only when an image was reproduced in a book, a magazine, or other print media.[18] Much younger than Kimura, Moriyama Daidō also treated his prints as "art for reproduction" (*shashin genkō*) until he had the first solo exhibition in 1974.[19] In a way, Japanese photographers during this period embraced the ultimate form of photography as a means of mass mechanical reproduction, as posited by Walter Benjamin in his famous treatise.[20]

Even when the artists owned the documentary photographs, the pictures tended to remain "reference materials" (*shiryō*). That is to say they were rarely made into "works" (*sakuhin*) as such. These photographs thus long evaded commodification, in marked contrast to Euro-American conceptual and performance art. It is only recently that an increasing effort has been made to historicize 1960s art by turning *shiryō* photographs into some sort of commodified form (such as editions of a portfolio). In some cases, artists have taken it upon themselves to intervene personally in such history-making. One important example is GUN's portfolio, produced in 2009, of its snow-painting event.

Against this less-than-perfect situation surrounding photography in art, Nomura established a new standard with *Tardiology*. By photographing the changing state of his work himself, he unambiguously retained the rights to the photographs he shot and thus claimed full authorship of both the process-based form-making *and* the photography. Ever inquisitive and analytical, Nomura closely scrutinized his photographs—as can be inferred from his interview—and came to realize that they were not mere documentation but "work" that could be shown as such in an exhibition. This is the crucial point that eluded other artists who depended on professional photographers to work for them, and even those (most notably Gutai) who retained control of the images but only as reference materials and art for reproduction. Nomura's training in sculpture might have helped him to objectify the process, separating it from his own acts (such as building the cardboard structure or moving the dry ice again and again).

In the works that followed *Tardiology*, Nomura took the logical step of showing his photographs of *Dryice* and *Iodine* in exhibitions. In them, fugitive materiality was the focus

Figure 13. Hirata Minoru, Hi Red Center's *Cleaning Event*, 1964. Documentary photograph of performance

of attention, not as a by-product but a main focus of the time-based process. His photographs were no precious commodity, however, and their preservation was not intended. They were printed on a type of paper used by television art departments to create background scenery. By definition, this fake scenery was disposable, discarded after filming. This trick, which he picked up through his day job at the broadcast company, allowed him to print his images large enough to create a room-size installation. Although he followed, whether knowingly or not, the custom among Japanese photographers to disregard the concept of "original prints," his prints were singularly meant for an exhibition, not for a publication. This also separated him from Japanese photographers, professional and amateurs alike.

As a pioneer of photo-based artworks, Nomura felt a tremendous amount of uncertainty about the legitimacy of his practice. His trepidation back then, as he expresses in his interview, is not easy to comprehend today, when the use of photography has become commonplace among contemporary artists. It was Nakahara Yūsuke who recognized the import of Nomura's practice when he came to give a public critique at the *Kyoto Independent Exhibition* in March 1970; there Nomura exhibited his photographs of *Dryice* for the first time. Nakahara, who traveled Europe and America to research his *Tokyo Biennale 1970*, must have been familiar with Western photo-based works—which Nomura could also have seen on the pages of such contemporary art magazines as *Bijutsu techō* (Art notebook). Still, it would have been almost unthinkable for Nomura, who was accustomed to seeing "documentary" photographs reproduced in the art media, to understand that those Euro-American photo-based works were intended for exhibition display. Thus, Nakahara's endorsement at the public critique in Kyoto, followed by his inclusion of Nomura's work in his own exhibition, was another crucial step in Nomura's progress.

Marketplaces in the Culture of Showing

If the culture of showing was dissociated from the art market, it did not follow that there was little support for artists in 1960s Japan. When showing was their priority, what counted more as support than the art market was having places for display. A particularly dynamic period of change, the expanded 1960s saw a fundamental shift in terms of the artists' marketplace, with the dividing point being January 1964, when the termination of the *Yomiuri Independent Exhibition* was announced.

The end of Yomiuri's exhibition meant the loss of a major official display space for Anti-Art, which was partly responsible for the shift toward Non-Art. Artist-generated sites of operation included small group exhibitions by like-minded colleagues, the artist-initiated independent exhibition movement, and non-exhibition venues for performative and conceptualist works (streets, landscapes, and mail, among others). The first option was made possible by a growing number of "rental galleries" (*kashi garō*), which have constituted a vital building block in Japan's art world, functioning as a marketplace for display that artists could always count on. These "facilities for one-shot exhibitions,"[21] may be frowned upon by dealers and museum curators, but in the culture of showing, the rental galleries were an indispensable and invaluable asset. Furthermore, certain respected rental galleries never just rented a space to anybody willing to pay the fee but often rigorously screened applying artists and sometimes organized their own exhibitions. In a way, they were tantamount to alternative spaces as we know them today. In Kyoto, where Nomura was active, Galerie 16 opened in 1962 as the city's first rental gallery specializing in contemporary art. When *Tokyo Biennale 1970* traveled to Kyoto, the Kyoto Municipal Museum of Art became a hub of visiting artists from Europe and America, including Daniel Buren, Hans Haacke, Mario Merz, and Richard Serra.[22] From 1970 through the 1990s, it also offered opportunities to Nomura to present his key works, including his '*moon*' *score* series.

Despite the shock caused by Yomiuri's termination, the official sites for display of contemporary art expanded greatly in the post-Yomiuri years. Two museums were added to support modern and contemporary art. One was the National Museum of Modern Art, Kyoto (established in a temporary space in 1962 and fully opened in 1967), which launched an annual survey, entitled *Trends in Contemporary Japanese Art / Gendai bijutsu no dōkō*, that lasted through 1970. The other was the private Museum of Contemporary Art, Nagaoka in Niigata Prefecture (inaugurated in 1964), which had an annual competition to

Figure 14. Hirata Minoru, *Anti-Expo Event*, Anti-Expo Group (with Zero Dimension and Kokuin), on the rooftop of Kyoto University's lecture hall, 1969. Documentary photograph of performance

Figure 15. The Play, *Voyage: A Happening in an Egg*, 1968. Documentary photograph of performance

"proactively contribute to the advancement of *gendai bijutsu*."[23] Yomiuri's role was replaced by Mainichi, another nationwide daily newspaper, which had had two contemporary exhibition programs since the 1950s. In 1962, Mainichi decided to expand its *Contemporary Art Exhibition of Japan / Gendai Nihon bijutsu-ten* by adding an open-call competitive section, which was not as freewheeling as Yomiuri's independent exhibition but encouraged vanguard artists to participate. In addition, Mainichi updated the English title of its *International Art Exhibition, Japan / Nihon kokusai bijutsu-ten* as *Tokyo Biennale* in 1965. These moves paved the way for *Tokyo Biennale 1970*, the critical success of which brought about more visibility and legitimacy for *gendai bijutsu* in the domestic art world and engendered a contact point with the international art world.

It was into this changing landscape that Nomura emerged with *Tardiology*. A pioneer of Non-Art, however, he helped shape his environment, while clearly benefiting from it. His operational environment cannot be properly contextualized without the study of Kyoto as a vital center of contemporary art. His schooling in Kyoto was a significant biographical factor. Founded in 1880 as the Kyoto-Prefecture Painting School (Kyoto-fu Gagakkō), his alma mater, Kyoto City University of Arts (Kyoto Shiritsu Geijutsu Daigaku), was historically a progressive school. In 1970, it was the first art school to create a course for contemporary art, which it called *kōsō sekkei* (conception and planning), in the aftermath of a campus conflict that resulted in extensive curriculum reform, including this new course.[24] Although Nomura completed his master's degree immediately before the student movement hit his school, its progressive attitude was felt when Nomura's *Tardiology* was presented at the Kyoto Municipal Museum of Art, together with other students' graduation projects. As he recalls in his interview, when the museum tried to remove his work, it was Tsuji Shindō, the head of the sculpture department, who defended his student. Because the museums—notably the Tokyo Metropolitan Art Museum—had been routinely at odds with experimentation by vanguard artists since the time of the *Yomiuri Independent Exhibition*, the Kyoto museum's complaint merely added to Nomura's vanguard credentials. What should not be overlooked here, however, is Tsuji's modernist standing. He was not an academician specializing in bronze statues, but a ceramic sculptor whose own abstract works with a slight hint of figuration were included in *The New Japanese Painting and Sculpture*, a landmark exhibition at the Museum of Modern Art, New York, in 1966.[25]

After *Tardiology*, Nomura first staged *Dryice* in October–November 1969 at the second *Exhibition of Contemporary Plastic Art / Gendai no zōkei*, held on the banks of the Kamo

River in Kyoto. During the monthlong exhibition, he spent every Sunday (October 19 and 26, November 2 and 9) and one national holiday (November 3) creating five iterations of the dry ice's evaporation, using different materials such as cardboard, rubber sheet, and canvas. The photographs of the rubber-sheet version (November 2) were then shown at the *Kyoto Independent Exhibition*, together with another photographic work, *Time on a Curved Line*. This caught the eye of Nakahara, who was actively scouting artists to include in *Tokyo Biennale 1970*. The *Kyoto Independent Exhibition* was one of the few successful regional independent exhibitions, established in 1955 and lasting through 1990.[26] Nomura himself was a semi-regular in the 1970s.

In addition to the independent exhibition, Kyoto offered valuable marketplaces for contemporary artists in the early 1970s, when similar opportunities seemingly dried up in Tokyo—ironically, due to the poor attendance at the critically provocative *Tokyo Biennale 1970*. Not only did the city museum organize the *Kyoto Biennale* in 1972, 1973, and 1976 (all of which included Nomura); it also hosted the fifth and sixth *Exhibition of Contemporary Plastic Art*, the annual exhibition series held at a few different venues over years. Nomura himself participated from the first exhibition, in 1968, through the seventh, in 1974. It is notable that the series radically shifted its attention from outdoor sculpture to the artist's films beginning with the third exhibition, in 1970, as though it trailed Nomura's interests. These Kyoto exhibitions were regularly reviewed by the contemporary art magazine *Bijutsu techō* (Art notebook), which signals their importance.

A comparison of Kyoto and Tokyo is fertile ground to examine as a way of understanding the expanded 1960s in Japanese art. Although that goes beyond the scope of this essay, quickly comparing Nomura and Sekine Nobuo illuminates the inherently contemporary nature of Kyoto's art world. Based in Tokyo, Sekine was a painting major who accidentally became a sculptor.[27] His high-relief painting was mistakenly accepted in the sculpture competition of Mainichi's contemporary exhibition in 1968, and he won a second prize, which led to the legendary *Phase—Mother Earth* that fall. Sekine stopped his Mono-ha practice, however, and turned to public sculpture in 1973. In doing so, he admirably sought to establish a connection between his art and society. It was a bold move for a contemporary artist at the time—prefiguring the community-based art projects proliferating in twenty-first-century Japan—even though the path he pursued was a rather traditional kind in the history of sculpture. In contrast, Nomura, a sculpture major, has continued to "sculpt time" by devising ever more innovative ways to look at our world—indeed, a whole spectrum of cosmology.

Notes

All translations from the Japanese are by the author.

I would like to thank Nomura Hitoshi for discussing his works with me over time. I am particularly indebted to Fergus McCaffrey for sharing his ideas and expertise with me from the earliest stage of preparing this essay. I still recall an exciting moment in 1999 when I first learned of his passion for the art of Nomura at the Queens Museum of Art, where I included two key works by the artist in the Japanese section of *Global Conceptualism*. I have also benefited from the research assistance of Professor Kimura Shigenobu, as well as Hirata Minoru and Hosoya Shūhei, Horikawa Michio, Ikemizu Keiichi, Kawaguchi Tatsuo and his son Yūki, Sakagami Shinogu, and Sekine Nobuo.

1. Nomura, interview with Reiko Tomii, April 2, 1996.

2. The French word *objet*, pronounced *obuje* in Japanese, was adopted into the Japanese art lexicon to denote (1) found everyday objects, (2) mainly three-dimensional works incorporating such objects, and, in a popularized form, (3) three-dimensional works that depart from conventional sculptural expressions.

3. I have argued for the need to have nuanced contextualized readings of "similar yet dissimilar" works in "'International Contemporaneity' in the 1960s: Discoursing on Art in Japan and Beyond," *Japan Review*, no. 21 (2009), 123–47; http://shinku.nichibun.ac.jp/jpub/pdf/jr/JN2103.pdf (accessed July 15, 2010).

4. For this terminology, see Tomii, "International Contemporaneity," and Reiko Tomii, "Historicizing 'Contemporary Art': Some Discursive Practices in *Gendai Bijutsu* in Japan," *Positions* 12, no. 3 (Winter 2004), 611–41.

5. For the discursive aspect of 1960s Japan, see Tomii, "Historicizing," and Reiko Tomii, "*Geijutsu* on Their Minds: Memorable Words on Anti-Art," in *Art, Anti-Art, Non-Art: Experimentations in the Public Sphere in Postwar Japan, 1950–1970*, ed. Charles Merewether and Rika Iezumi Hiro (Los Angeles: Getty Research Institute, 2007), 35–62.

6. For this periodization, see Reiko Tomii, "'Art Outside the Box' in 1960s Japan: An Introduction and Commentary," *Review of Japanese Culture and Society* (Saitama, Japan: Jōsai University) 17 (December 2005), 5.

7. See Ashiya City Museum of Art and History, ed., *Gutai shiryōshū / Document Gutai, 1954–1972* (Ashiya: Ashiya City Culture Foundation, 1993); and Hirai Shōichi, ed., *"Gutai" tte nanda? / What's Gutai?* (Tokyo: Bijutsu Shuppan-sha, 2004).

8. Ushio Shinohara, *Zen'ei no michi* [The avant-garde road] (Tokyo: Bijutsu Shuppan-sha, 1968), 78.

9. William Klein, *Tokyo* (New York: Crown Publishers, 1964).

10. See Akasegawa Genpei, *Tokyo mikisā keikaku: Hai Reddo Sentā chokusetsu kōdō no kiroku* [Tokyo mixer plans: Documents of Hi Red Center] (Tokyo: Chikuma Shobō, 1985).

11. See Hirata Minoru, *Katō Yoshihiro to 60-nendai / Zero Dimension: Yoshihiro Kato and 60's* (Tokyo: Kawade Shobō Shinsha, 2006); and KuroDalaiJee (Kuroda Raiji), "The Rituals of 'Zero Jigen' in Urban Space," *R*, no. 2 (2003), 27–32; www.kanazawa21.jp/tmpImages/videoFiles/file-52-2-e-file-2.pdf (accessed July 15, 2010).

12. See Reiko Tomii, "After the 'Descent to the Everyday': Japanese Collectivism from Hi Red Center to The Play, 1964–1973," in *Collectivism After Modernism*, ed. Blake Stimson and Gregory Sholette (Minneapolis: University of Minnesota Press, 2007), 44–75; and *GUN Group: Event to Change the Image of Snow* (Tokyo: Tokyo Gallery, 2009).

13. Akasegawa Genpei, *Han-geijutsu Anpan* [Anti-Art independent exhibition] (1985); pocketbook edition (Tokyo: Chikuma Bunko, 1994), 216.

14. Akasegawa, *Han-geijutsu Anpan*, 110–11.

15. Akasegawa, *Han-geijutsu Anpan*, 216–17.

16. For these incidents involving Shiraga, see Reiko Tomii, "Shiraga Paints: Toward a 'Concrete' Discussion," in *Kazuo Shiraga: Six Decades*, exh. cat. (New York: McCaffrey Fine Art, 2009), 9–30.

17. See *Miyazaki Junnosuke*, exh. cat. (Fukuoka: Fukuoka Art Museum, 1998), 21.

18. Kaneko Ryūichi and Ivan Vartanian, *Japanese Photobooks of the 1960s and '70s* (New York: Aperture, 2009), 166.

19. Moriyama Daidō, "Photography in Print," in Kaneko and Vartanian, *Japanese Photobooks*, 26–27; Moriyama's reference to the 1974 exhibition appears only in the Japanese edition, *Nihon shashinshū-shi 1956–1986* [The history of Japanese photobooks, 1956–1986] (Tokyo: Akaaka, 2009), 26.

20. Walter Benjamin, "The Work of Art in the Age of Mechanical Reproduction" (1936), in *Illuminations*, trans. Harry Zohn (New York: Schocken Books, 1969).

21. Quoted from William S. Lieberman's introduction to *The New Japanese Painting and Sculpture*, exh. cat. (New York: The Museum of Modern Art, 1966), 9–10.

22. Inoue Michiko et al. (roundtable discussion), "40-nenkan no bijutsu no nagare to kongo no tenkai" [40 years of contemporary art and the future direction], brochure accompanying a two-CD compilation, *40 Years of Galerie 16* (Kyoto: Galerie 16, 2003), 1, 7.

23. "Goaisatsu" [Greetings], in *Nagaoka Gendai Bijutsukan-shō kaikoten 1964–1968* [A retrospective of the Museum of Contemporary Art, Nagaoka, Prize Exhibition 1964–1968], exh. cat. (Niigata: The Niigata Prefectural Museum of Modern Art et al., 2002), n.p.

24. See Kimura Shigenobu, "Geidai 50-shūnen o mukaete no kaisō: Gakusei kaikaku to iten mondai" [Recollections on the occasion of the Art University's 50th anniversary: Curriculum reform and campus relocation], in *Kimura Shigenobu chosakushū, dai-8-kan: Seikatsu bunka ron* [Writings by Kimura Shigenobu, vol. 8, On life and culture] (Tokyo: Shibunkaku, 2004), 134–40; and Oral History Interview with Kimura Shigenobu, conducted by Reiko Tomii and Ikegami Hiroko, May 25, 2010, Oral History Archives of Japanese Art (www.oralarthistory.org, forthcoming).

25. *The New Japanese Painting and Sculpture*, 32–33.

26. *Kyoto-shi Bijutsukan 40-nen shi* [Four decades of Kyoto Municipal Museum of Art] (Kyoto: Kyoto Municipal Museum of Art, 1974), 63–69.

27. For Sekine's career path, see Reiko Tomii, "How *Gendai Bijutsu* Stole the 'Museum': An Institutional Observation of the Vanguard 1960s," in *Japanese Art of the Modern Age* [provisional title], ed. Tom Rimer (Honolulu: University of Hawai'i Press, forthcoming in 2011–12).

Figure 16. Nomura Hitoshi installing *Liquid Nitrogen: −196° C*, 1971

Selected Chronology

1945
January: Nomura Hitoshi is born in Hyogo Prefecture, Japan.

1963
April: Enters Kyoto City University of Arts, joining the Department of Sculpture, where Nomura studies under Professors Tsuji Shindō and Horiuchi Masakazu.

1967
April: Enters the Graduate School of Kyoto City University of Arts.

1969
March: Presents *Tardiology*, an eight-meter-tall cardboard box sculpture that collapses under its own weight, in the *Graduate Works* exhibition at Kyoto Municipal Museum of Art, and completes his graduate course in sculpture at Kyoto City University of Arts.
April: Starts work at a television broadcast company.

1970
March: Takes part in the *Kyoto Independent Exhibition* at Kyoto Municipal Museum of Art, presenting the photographic works *Dryice* and

Time on a Curved Line. These works attract the attention of Nakahara Yūsuke, who decides to include Nomura's work in the *10th International Art Exhibition of Japan (Tokyo Biennale)* during May.
April: Holds his first solo exhibition, *Iodine and Time Table*, at Galerie 16, Kyoto.
May: Participates in the *10th International Art Exhibition of Japan—Between Man and Matter* at Tokyo Metropolitan Art Museum, which features the work of forty artists from around the world.

1972
March: Begins work on *Photobook or The Brownian Motion of Eyesight*, using a 16mm movie camera (it is discontinued after ten years, in February 1982).

1975
September: Participates in the 9th *Biennale de Paris* at Musée National d'Art Moderne, Paris, and Musée National d'Art Moderne de la Ville de Paris.
December: Realizing that the moon seen through power cables resembles a music score, Nomura begins photographing the *'moon' score* series (which is ongoing).

Figure 17. Nomura Hitoshi, freshman year at college, 1963

Figure 18. Nomura Hitoshi after cutting a record in Paris, 1975

Figure 19. Nomura Hitoshi, working at a broadcasting firm, ca. 1970–73

1976
January: At the solo exhibition *A Special Room for HEARING* at Galerie 16, Kyoto, Nomura reconstructs the recording and transcription process used to capture everyday conversations for the creation of *Hearing* during the previous year.

1978
August: Places a camera on an equatorial telescope to photograph the center of the Milky Way and captures the Pleiades cluster, which shines with a blue light in the eastern sky. The mountains in the foreground of these images appear blurred, inspiring the *Earth Rotation* series, which Nomura commences in December and concludes in November of the following year.

1979
Releases the LP recording *'moon' score*.

1980
March: Begins work on *A Spin in Curved Air* series, using a fisheye lens to record the passage of the sun through the sky over the course of a day (continued until December 1988). This work provides the inspiration for a later work, *The Sun on Latitude 35° N* (1982–87).

1982
March: After participating in the 5th *India Triennial* in New Delhi, Nomura visits various sites connected to Shakyamuni Buddha.

Begins *The Sun on Latitude 35° N*, which is completed in 1987 after five years of work.

1983
May: Nomura encounters the musical score for Bach's Suite for Cello and notes how it resembles birds flying. This leads him to start work on the *'birds' score* series, in which birds in flight are double-exposed on top of a musical staff (an ongoing series).
November: Obtains his first meteors. One resembles the Zen priest Bodhidharma, sitting in front of a wall in deep meditation, and another the figure of Buddha, with a robe billowing outward as he walked. Nomura becomes fascinated by the mysterious creative power of the universe, referring to it as a "cosmic sensibility," and subsequently begins to use meteors in his work.

1984
Nomura has been photographing the waterfall at Nachi in Wakayama Prefecture since 1982, but begins traveling there more regularly to photograph the waterfall with stars and the sun, creating the works in the *Spin & Gravity* series.

1985
While photographing the sun, Nomura notices that the shadow of a lightning conductor does not fall due north at noon, and he thereby realizes that a discrepancy exists between clock time and the movements of the sun. He discovers that the time it takes for the sun to rotate around the celestial sphere is not exactly twenty-four hours, a phenomenon known as the "equation of time." This inspires Nomura to record the sun's position at the same time every day over the course of a year to create the *Analemma* series.

1987
July: *Recent Works 2: Nomura Hitoshi—Spin & Gravity* at the National Museum of Modern Art, Osaka.

1988
February: Presents *Time Arrow: Liquid Nitrogen –196° C*, using liquid oxygen and nitrogen in a two-person show with Murata Chiaki entitled *Is Temperature a Fundamental Factor of Substance?* at ABC Gallery, Osaka.
October: Ceases work at the broadcast company, where he had been employed for almost twenty years, to become an assistant professor at Kyoto City University of Arts.

1989
September: Releases the CD *'moon' score (hv/010)*.

1990
September–November: Participates in *Japanese Art of the 1980's*, Frankfurter Kunstverein, Frankfurt; Museum of Modern Art, Vienna.

1991

October–December: Participates in *A Cabinet of Signs*, Tate Gallery Liverpool.

1992

January–May: *A Cabinet of Signs*, Whitechapel Art Gallery, London; Malmö Konsthall, Sweden.
December 9–25: Visits the Hamelin Pool in Australia to photograph stromatolites. Confronted by these primeval forms, Nomura ponders the connection and relationship between inorganic and living matter.

1993

May: Establishes the Solar Power Lab (SPL) and creates *Sun Structure '93*, a solar-powered car, thereafter producing one annually until 1999.

1994

August: Publication of *Time-Space: Hitoshi Nomura*, by Korinsha Press; release of the CD *'birds' score*.

1995

January: *Nomura Hitoshi: Change over Time*, Spiral Garden, Tokyo.
May: Begins plotting the route for a solar car to traverse the United States. *Nomura Hitoshi: Chronoscore*, Tokyo Metropolitan Museum of Photography.

1996

Participates in *Photography and Beyond in Japan: Space, Time and Memory*, Vancouver Art Gallery, Vancouver; Los Angeles County Museum, Los Angeles; Corcoran Gallery of Art, Washington, D.C.; and Denver Art Museum, Denver.
April: Is elected professor at Kyoto City University of Arts.
August: The solar car *Sun Structure '96* takes third place in the 800 Watt Class at the Solar Power Grand Prix, Suzuka.
November: Exhibits *Soft Landing Meteor & DNA* at Gallery GAN, Tokyo.

1997

August: *Sun Structure '97* wins the 800 Watt Class at the Solar Power Grand Prix, Suzuka.

1999

July 15–September 4: With ten members of the SPL, Nomura traverses the United States, completing *HAAS Project—Harnessing the Sun: A Journey Across America by Solar Car*.

2000

January: In response to the Shuttle Radar Topography Mission (SRTM) by the Space Shuttle STS-99, Nomura carries out the *Space Shuttle + Daimonji Project*.
April: With the establishment of a doctoral course at Kyoto City University of Arts, Nomura becomes a professor and chief instructor at the graduate school.
August: *Nomura Hitoshi—Genesis of Life: The Universe, the Sun, DNA*, at Contemporary Art Center, Art Tower Mito, Ibaraki.

2001

June: *Nomura Hitoshi—Transit/Reflect* at the Toyota Municipal Museum of Art.

2002

March: Begins construction of observation equipment for *The Analemma*.
August: Carries out research with NASDA (now JAXA), Japan's space development agency, and visits NASA to participate in interviews with Japanese astronauts Noguchi Soichi, Wakata Koichi, Mukai Chiaki, and Doi Takao.

2003

May: Begins work on *Octopusic Conversation: Chromatist*.
July: In order to identify the movements of the sun over a four-year period, including a leap year, Nomura once again begins to photograph *The Analemma* (an ongoing series).
September: Using an oblong musical staff, Nomura produces the musical score and DVD *Elliptic Score: In Falling*.

2004

January: Photographs cranes on the Izumi Plain in Kagoshima Prefecture.

2006

August: *Sparkling Neurons (Cosmic Rays Hitting Neurons)* and *'moon' score: ISS Astronaut* are selected for the ISS/Kibo Cultural and Humanistic Science Utilization, a pilot mission for the application of cultural and social sciences.
September: *Hitoshi Nomura: An Introduction, Photoworks 1975–91* at McCaffrey Fine Art, New York.
October: *Seeing: Contingency and Necessity. The Work of Hitoshi Nomura* is published by Akaaka Art Publishing, and the CD *'Grus' score (hv/110)* is released.

2007

July: Long fascinated with Palaeozoic plants, which preceded animal life on land, Nomura acquires a sample of *Chara fragilis*, which is said to be the forerunner of terrestrial plant life.
September: Examining the influence of different frequencies of light on the cultivation of plant life, Nomura exhibits *Plants Are Chromatists, Unending Since Emergence*, in the exhibition *Nomura Hitoshi—Chrono & Chroma* at Art Court Gallery, Osaka.

2009

March: Participates in *Waiting for Video: Works from the 1960s to Today* at the National Museum of Modern Art, Tokyo.
April: *'moon' score: ISS Astronaut's Moon* is photographed by the astronaut Wakata Kōichi.
May: *Nomura Hitoshi: Perceptions—Changes in Time and Field* at the National Art Center, Tokyo.
December: *Hitoshi Nomura: View from Space, From Here On . . ."* at Art Court Gallery, Osaka.

2010

September: *Hitoshi Nomura: Marking Time* at McCaffrey Fine Art, New York.

Public Collections

Chiba City Museum of Art
Dallas Museum of Art
Getty Research Institute, Los Angeles
International Center of Photography, New York
Kawaguchi Museum of Contemporary Art
Kitakyushu Municipal Museum of Art
Kyoto Municipal Museum of Art
Meguro Museum of Art, Tokyo
Museum of Fine Arts, Gifu
Museum of Modern Art, New York
Museum of Modern Art, Saitama
Museum of Modern Art, Shiga
Museum of Modern Art, Wakayama
National Museum of Art, Osaka
National Museum of Modern Art, Kyoto
National Museum of Modern Art, Tokyo
San Francisco Museum of Modern Art
Tochigi Prefectural Museum of Fine Arts

Acknowledgments

I first encountered the work of Nomura Hitoshi as a research scholar at Kyoto University, Japan, in 1994. The shock and wonder I experienced then remains undiminished more than fifteen years later as we publish the first monograph in English on his diverse and challenging work. And on this occasion, there are many to whom I would like to extend my deepest gratitude.

First and foremost, I must thank Nomura Hitoshi for his extraordinary art and his faith in me as a gallerist. McCaffrey Fine Art's first exhibition was a solo show of Nomura-sensei's work, and it was from that successful acorn that we have grown. I must also especially single out Keiko Omura, whose dedication, generosity, and support for Nomura-sensei and me have been unparalleled. Truly this exhibition and publication would not exist without your assistance; thank you, Keiko.

We are pleased to note that a number of art historians, critics, and curators have played a vital role in bringing this project to fruition. In particular, I would like to thank Martha Buskirk for her insightful essay placing Nomura in the context of his international peers. And I must also thank Reiko Tomii for her essay and her work in general on postwar Japanese art.

In preparing the exhibition, Watanabe Shinya, Tetsuya Yamazaki and his staff at Pranayama Art, and Bruce Dow have been indispensible. We also are grateful to Toyonaga Seiji, Nomura Takuro, and Robert Moeller.

I would also like to thank the following individuals for their early advocacy of Nomura's work in the United States: Allan Schwartzman, Sandra Phillips, Alexandra Munroe & Robert Rosenkranz, Barbara London, Jeffrey Hoffeld, Christopher Dark, and Sandy Heller. In addition, I must acknowledge the long support provided by Yagi Mitsue to Nomura-sensei over the last twenty years in Japan.

Thank you to the following for their assistance with documentation, illustrations, and research: Professor Kimura Shigenobu, as well as Hirata Minoru and Hosoya Shūhei, Ikemizu Keiichi of The Play, Kawaguchi Tatsuo of Group "I" and his son Yūki of Relation Bridge, and Sekine Nobuo.

Lisa Panzera organized the production of this volume, heading the McCaffrey Fine Art team in New York with the assistance of Nina Stojkovic. Special thanks to Richard Slovak, who provided sage editorial advice. And finally, Miko McGinty and Rita Jules must be commended for their outstanding work in producing an exceptional publication.

FMC

Author Biographies

MARTHA BUSKIRK is Professor of Art History and Criticism at Montserrat College of Art in Beverly, Massachusetts, where she has taught since 1994. She is the author of *The Contingent Object of Contemporary Art* (MIT Press, 2003) and is currently working on a new book, *Seeing through the Museum: Art, Life, Commerce*. She is also co-editor of *The Duchamp Effect* (MIT Press, 1996) with Mignon Nixon, as well as *The Destruction of Tilted Arc: Documents* (MIT Press, 1990) with Clara Weyergraf-Serra. Buskirk earned her Ph.D. in art history from the City University of New York Graduate Center, and she held fellowships at the Radcliffe Institute for Advanced Study in 2000–2001, the Clark Art Institute in 2004, and the Henry Moore Institute in 2006.

REIKO TOMII is an independent scholar and curator whose work is focused on postwar Japanese art within global and local contexts. Her co-curated exhibitions include *Global Conceptualism* (Queens Museum of Art, 1999) and *Century City* (Tate Modern, 2001). She authored *Kazuo Shiraga: Six Decades* (McCaffrey Fine Art, 2009) and co-authored (with Eric C. Shiner) *Making a Home: Japanese Contemporary Artists in New York* (Japan Society, 2007). In addition, she has contributed to *Collectivism after Modernism* (University of Minnesota Press, 2007), *Art, Anti-Art, Non-Art* (Getty Research Institute, 2007), and *Xu Bing* (forthcoming). A co-founder of PoNJA-GenKon, a Listserv group of specialists interested in contemporary Japanese art, Tomii holds a Ph.D. in art history from the University of Texas at Austin.

This volume accompanies the exhibition *Hitoshi Nomura: Marking Time*, presented at McCaffrey Fine Art, New York, from September 15 through October 23, 2010.

Editor: Richard Slovak
Associate Editor: Lisa Panzera
Designers: Rita Jules and Gerard Mullin, Miko McGinty Inc.
Typeset in Sabon
Printed and bound by Trifolio, S.R.L., Verona, Italy

Front cover: Nomura Hitoshi installing *Liquid Nitrogen: −196° C*, 1971. Liquid nitrogen, cardboard. 10 sheets, 15¾ x 10⅞ inches (40 x 27.5 cm) each
Back cover: *Tardiology* (detail), 1968–69. From a sequence of 8 black-and-white photographs. 2 photos, 31½ x 47¼ inches (80 x 120 cm) each (image size); 4 photos, 47¼ x 31½ inches (120 x 80 cm) each (image size); 2 photos, 31½ x 47¼ inches (80 x 120 cm) each (image size)
Frontispiece: *Iodine* (detail), March 29, 1970. From a sequence of 12 black-and-white photographs. 27⅝ x 33⅞ inches (70 x 86 cm) each (image size)

ISBN-13: 978-0-9790484-5-6